# Smarter
# Pricing

**FT** Prentice Hall
FINANCIAL TIMES

In an increasingly competitive world, we believe it's quality of thinking that will give you the edge – an idea that opens new doors, a technique that solves a problem, or an insight that simply makes sense of it all. The more you know, the smarter and faster you can go.

That's why we work with the best minds in business and finance to bring cutting-edge thinking and best learning practice to a global market.

Under a range of leading imprints, including *Financial Times Prentice Hall*, we create world-class print publications and electronic products bringing our readers knowledge, skills and understanding which can be applied whether studying or at work.

To find out more about Pearson Education publications, or tell us about the books you'd like to find, you can visit us at
**www.pearsoned.co.uk**

# Smarter Pricing

How to capture more value in your market

Tony Cram

 Prentice Hall
FINANCIAL TIMES

*An imprint of* **Pearson Education**

London • New York • Toronto • Sydney • Tokyo • Singapore • Hong Kong
Cape Town • New Delhi • Madrid • Paris • Amsterdam • Munich • Milan

PEARSON EDUCATION LIMITED

Edinburgh Gate
Harlow CM20 2JE
Tel: +44 (0)1279 623623
Fax: +44 (0)1279 431059
Website: www.pearsoned.co.uk

First published in Great Britain in 2006

© Pearson Education Limited 2006

The right of Tony Cram to be identified as author of this work has been asserted
by him in accordance with the Copyright, Designs and Patents Act 1988.

ISBN-13: 987-0-273-70613-7
ISBN-10: 0-273-70613-6

*British Library Cataloguing in Publication Data*
A catalogue record for this book is available from the British Library

*Library of Congress Cataloging in Publication Data*
A catalog record for this book is available from the Library of Congress

10 9 8 7 6 5 4 3 2
10 09 08 07 06

Designed by Sue Lamble
Typeset in 9.5pt Stone Serif by 70
Printed in Great Britain by Henry Ling Ltd., at the Dorset Press, Dorchester, Dorset

*The Publisher's policy is to use paper manufactured from sustainable forests.*

For Joe, Ben, Jessica and Peter

# Contents

# Acknowledgements

My first acknowledgement goes to the many authors and great minds behind the books, articles and publications listed under 'Going further – references and additional reading' at the end of most chapters in this book. Three books in particular sparked my original interest in the subject of pricing and my thanks go to Thomas T. Nagle and Reed K. Holden for *The Strategy and Tactics of Pricing*, to Robert J. Dolan and Hermann Simon for *Power Pricing* and finally to Michael V. Marn, Eric V. Roegner and Craig C. Zawada of McKinsey & Company for *The Price Advantage*. Any reader wishing to go further should begin with these books. I have also drawn inspiration from the many pricing articles published in the *McKinsey Quarterly*.

Second, I must recognize the contribution of the Master of Business Administration (MBA) classes at Ashridge Business School. They ever impress with their ability to pose challenging questions about pricing and throw new light on the issues under discussion. Perhaps their enthusiasm for this demanding subject led me to go further.

Third, I owe thanks to James Pickford of the *Financial Times* who invited me to capture current thinking in an article for his newspaper, published in August 2004. As a result of this article, Richard Stagg of Pearson Education called me and the conversation led to this book. Throughout the project, Richard has given me timely encouragement and well-founded support. The editorial guidance I received from Benjamin Roberts was perceptive and motivating. I enjoyed working with him.

I was eager to build on the ideas of the best thinkers on pricing and so my fourth acknowledgement goes to Lorraine Oliver and Rachel Piper who were diligent and creative in their research on my behalf. Celia Tucker advised on cover design. Thanks to the whole team at the Ashridge Learning Resource Centre.

Chris Cram worked with me to define the scope of the book and determine its structure. She also researched and refined examples of good practice.

A number of practitioners gave me ideas and allowed me to use their published material. Particular thanks go to Jonas Gunnarsson of ICA, Cathy Billett of the AA and Janey Berry of Waitrose for permission to illustrate the book with their examples. Colleagues, friends and family members gave me their own perspectives on pricing and offered advice, examples and suggestions. Thanks to you all.

Final thanks go to Janet Smallwood, Joy Ashford and Elaine Stedman of Ashridge for freeing my time to work on this project.

## Publisher's acknowledgements

We are grateful to the following for permission to reproduce copyright material:

Waitrose for 'The Peculiar Incident of the Fishmonger Performing on Hilary's Table' advertisement; the Automobile Association for '£39 joining' press advertisement; *Financial Times* for use of 'UK dwelling costs' table (March 12 2005).

In some instances we may have been unable to trace the owners of copyright material, and we would appreciate any information that would enable us to do so.

# Upwards, not downwards

Some of your prices are too low.

Some customers would pay more, and there are times and places where you could charge more. Of course none of your customers will tell you this, though they are all too ready and eager to tell you when your prices are too high.

In the meantime, your competitors harangue your customers with promises of lower prices, and besiege you with price wars. On a daily basis, the media challenge profitable businesses and train their audiences to be price-sensitive bargain hunters.

All this price pressure goes one way: downwards.

There is another way. This book is aimed in the other direction, helping to move your customers and your business upwards. It will help you to understand the value delivered to your customers and show you how to increase it, how to communicate it and, most importantly, how you can capture an increased proportion of this value.

It is all about commanding the right price, and the right price is, more than you would imagine possible, a higher one.

This is smarter pricing.

# 1

# Pricing by voodoo or bingo? – there's a better way

For Lacoste, the aspirational clothing brand, it was tough selling across the USA in the 1990s. Customers were more demanding than ever. They had more choice. The competition in up-market clothing was intense. More spending on promotion and advertising affected margins. Costs were rising. The licence for the USA had been held in the 1980s by General Mills and, by the late 1990s, the crocodile logo appeared on shirts retailing for as little as $35. According to Jonah Bloom, writing in *Advertising Age*, this low price cheapened the brand and forced General Mills to cut costs to maintain margins, using inferior fabrics and manufacturing techniques. Poorer quality reduced sales putting further pressure on cost saving – a downward spiral.

What would you do?

When former Levi's executive, Robert Siegel, took over the loss-making brand in 2001, he was advised to cut prices to stimulate demand. In fact he took prices in the opposite direction, with restyled men's shirts increased to $69 and shapelier women's shirts up to $72. 'Part of the brand is the pricing', he said. 'Our quality is very high.' In his view, a cheaper sales tag would not reflect the quality, nor allow continued product investment. Sales in the USA rose 125 percent in 2004 and were forecast to increase 60 percent in 2005. In the luxury clothing market, higher prices contribute significantly to the aspirational positioning of the brand.

Pricing is important for the customer. The price positions a product more effectively and more convincingly than any other piece of communication – the € price of a Miele washing machine spells exclusive excellence, the price starburst on the Ryanair website cries 'no frills'. In a Belgian supermarket, faced with 20 unfamiliar brands of local beer, you can speedily identify the premium players, the mid-market brands and the bottom-rung products, simply by looking at the prices.

Advanced Micro Devices (AMD), the processor rival to brand leader Intel, launched its most expensive ever processor in summer 2005. They described the Athlon 64 FX-57 processor as the 'ultimate PC processor for PC gamers'. The processor was priced at $1,031, 25 percent higher than its predecessor the FX-55, though it only offered 7 percent more performance. More importantly, the comparable chip from Intel – the Pentium 4 Extreme Edition 3.730Ghz – costs only $999. The *Financial Times* explained this as 'a strategy by AMD to promote an image as a premium-priced supplier of high-end processors'.

Prices generate emotions. Low prices can lead to accusations of loss-making, dumping and being a cheapskate. More often, seemingly high prices result in charges of gouging, fleecing, unfairness and ripping-off. Yet when you pay 40 pence more per kilo for Fairtrade bananas you know the extra money goes to the growers and you feel positive about the product and even better about yourself. So much better that sales are rising across Europe. More than 20 percent of bananas sold in Switzerland are Fairtrade and UK sales rose over 40 percent in 2004.

Pricing is also important for the company. Price 'captures value' in the most direct way possible – a profitable return. The case is long proven. In 1992 a McKinsey survey by Marn and Rosiello covered 2,483 companies and calculated that a 1 percent increase in prices improves operating profit by 11.1 percent – greatly exceeding the impact of a 1 percent improvement in fixed costs (+2.3 percent), volume (+3.3 percent) or even variable costs (+7.8 percent).

Look at a property example. The London-based Home Builders Feder-ation (HBF) has estimated UK dwelling costs as shown in Table 1.1.

| Table 1.1 | UK dwelling costs | |
| --- | --- | --- |
| *Element* | *HBF % estimate* | *Costs for £200k house* |
| Land | 40% | £80,000 |
| Labour and construction | 30% | £60,000 |
| Planning and administration | 20% | £40,000 |
| Profit margin | 10% | £20,000 |

*Source*: *Financial Times*, 12 March 2005.

Hence, if a house-builder is able to persuade a buyer to pay £202,000 instead of £200,000 – an increase of just 1 percent – then profit increases by £2,000 or ten percentage points. The profit leverage of quite small price changes can be significant.

---

### case study 1.1

## How better prices made Caterpillar $250 million

**In April 2005,** Caterpillar Inc., the Illinois-based maker of industrial machinery and engines, reported a 38 percent jump in first quarter earnings. Net income rose to $581 million, or $1.63 a share, from $420 million, or $1.19 a share. Revenue grew to $8.34 billion, well above analysts' estimate of $7.3 billion. Caterpillar said the sales growth was led by $1.01 billion of higher machinery volume, $425 million of higher engine volume, $250 million of pricing moves, and the impact of foreign currency exchange, which contributed $102 million.

Merrill Lynch Global Securities Research observed that pricing power is a big factor in the optimism for company growth. Price increases, which Caterpillar said would average about 5.5 percent, compared to 2.4 percent last year, 'will become an increasingly important part of Caterpillar's story in the coming quarters and even more so in 2006', said Merrill Lynch.

> Jim Owens, Chairman and Chief Executive, said the higher 2005 outlook was the result of the 'fundamental strength' of its key markets. Caterpillar was well positioned to meet growth in demand from mining companies and an expanding number of infrastructure projects. Pricing decisions added $250 million to Caterpillar's profits.

Finding the right price has greater impact on market success than any other factor.

## It's important, so how well are we doing it?

Leading thinkers agree that pricing is poorly managed. Advertising guru, David Ogilvy, wrote in his book, *Ogilvy on Advertising*, that 'pricing is guesswork. It is usually assumed that marketers use scientific methods to determine the price of their products. Nothing could be further from the truth.' Harvard Marketing Professor, Robert J. Dolan, author of *Power Pricing: How managing price transforms the bottom line*, wrote that 'Pricing is the manager's biggest marketing headache. It's where they feel the most pressure to perform and the least certain that they are doing a good job.'

Pricing and marketing consultants, Simon Kucher and Partners, state that 'Price is the number one profit determinant. However, there is no other area in which, due to a lack of systematic analysis, such large profit potentials are left unrealized.' A 2003 report by the consultants McKinsey & Company suggested that 80–90 percent of poor pricing decisions featured under-pricing. Finally, Mark Ritson, London Business School's Assistant Professor of Marketing, pithily summarized the situation: 'Pricing is the worst managed of all marketing areas. How prices are decided is often a mixture of voodoo and bingo.'

If it is so important, why isn't it done better? The start of the challenge is the mass of data. Each sale of each item, to each customer, each week generates data. A wholesaler with 100,000 line items and 3,000 customers in different industries with different ordering patterns, would need a supercomputer to analyze the pricing impact of company sales statistics. It is like drinking from a fire-hydrant.

Added to this is the number of competitors, direct and indirect, whose actions may impact on the relative perceptions of customers. A commercial printer investigating firms who may bid for equivalent work could have to consider 40 rivals.

Another factor in the pricing equation is the margin effect of changing cost prices. There are 17 ingredients listed for a Knorr chicken stock cube and the company will have other costs to consider including labour, property, transport, insurance, packaging, marketing and merchandising.

Internally there are many players in the pricing process. The accounts department will identify costs; sales will consider customers; the marketing department will research consumers and competitors; the legal department will ensure regulatory compliance; production and distribution set supply constraints. Conflicting objectives need resolution when the finance department view on margin calls for higher prices and the sales team focus on revenue and share growth points to lower prices. According to McKinsey consultants, Eugster, Kakkar and Roegner, 'Companies often base prices on the anecdotal evidence of a few vocal sales people or product managers.'

Finally, it is hard to set measurable objectives for pricing. High prices are likely to mean lost sales. Low prices mean margin left on the table. The true measure of pricing is the minimization of profit foregone through under- or over-pricing – not easy to calibrate on a balanced scorecard.

As a result of these challenges (see Figure 1.1), many organizations silently delegate pricing decisions to their customers and competitors. They simply react to pressures and opportunities in the market place as they arise.

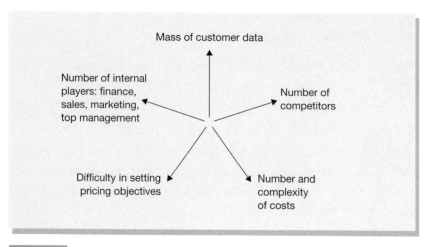

Figure 1.1    Challenges in setting prices

## Smarter pricing

There is a better way.

Smarter pricing begins with the customer and the potential customer (see Figure 1.2). Who are they? What do they need? What gives them value? What can they afford? How much are they willing to pay? How price sensitive are they? How could you influence this? Does price sensitivity vary between customer groups? What is the optimum combination of price and volume? How can you shape demand and customer behaviour?

Smarter pricing takes into account competitors and alternative ways customers could spend their money. What do you stand for relative to competitors? How are you differentiated? How can price support your positioning? How do you respond to value players? What tactics help you survive price wars? How will your prices influence the behaviour of competitors?

Smarter pricing responds to your company objectives. What is your desired role in the industry? What is your target positioning? What is your life-cycle pricing plan? How does the price deliver an adequate financial return? What price structure will best capture value? How can you move customers up price stairways?

Finally, smarter pricing keeps discipline and measures results.

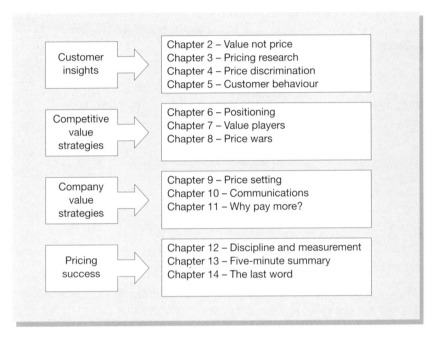

Customer insights → Chapter 2 – Value not price
Chapter 3 – Pricing research
Chapter 4 – Price discrimination
Chapter 5 – Customer behaviour

Competitive value strategies → Chapter 6 – Positioning
Chapter 7 – Value players
Chapter 8 – Price wars

Company value strategies → Chapter 9 – Price setting
Chapter 10 – Communications
Chapter 11 – Why pay more?

Pricing success → Chapter 12 – Discipline and measurement
Chapter 13 – Five-minute summary
Chapter 14 – The last word

**Figure 1.2**    Smarter pricing

## Chapter takeaways

■ Pricing positions products faster than any other element in the marketing mix.

■ It is the most important profit driver.

■ Experts believe that pricing is poorly managed with profit potential left unrealized.

■ Complexity is an explanation, encouraging organizations to be price-reactors. In effect they delegate pricing management to customers and competitors.

■ The recommendation is to price smarter.

## Management questions for your business

- How does price position our products?
- What emotions – positive and negative – do our prices encourage?
- How would a 1 percent across the board price increase impact our profits?
- How do we decide our prices?

## Going further – references and additional reading

Bloom, J. (2005) 'Lacoste's Siegel illustrates the sales power of pricing up', *Advertising Age*, 7 February.

Cram, T. (2004) 'Boost brand and profit with the right price', *Financial Times*, 6 August.

Dolan, R. J. and Simon, H. (1997) *Power Pricing: How managing price transforms the bottom line*, Simon & Schuster, New York, NY.

Eugster, C. E. Kakkar, J. N. and Roegner, E. V. (2000) 'Bringing discipline to pricing', *McKinsey Quarterly*, 1.

Fair trade bananas: www.bananalink.org.uk/future/future_2.htm and Prince, R. (2005) 'Savvy shopper', *Daily Telegraph*, 12 March.

Lester, T. (2002) 'How to ensure the price is exactly right', *Financial Times*, 30 January.

Marn, M. and Rosiello, R. L. (1992) 'Managing price, gaining profit', *Harvard Business Review*, September/October.

Nuttall, C. (2005), 'AMD to launch premium chip', *Financial Times*, 27 June.

Ogilvie, D. (1983) *Ogilvie on Advertising*, Pan, London.

Smy, L. (2005) 'Competition challenges builders to produce homes for £60,000', *Financial Times*, 12 March.

www.caterpillar.com

www.simon-kucher.com

# Customers: smarter ways to understand them

# 2

# When they say price, they really mean value

Smarter pricing begins by understanding that the customer is trading money for more than simply a product or service. Customers are buying a combination of product (or service) performance, plus an emotional association. For instance, DHL's express airfreight service competes with low-cost no-name shippers, but combined with the DHL service there is an emotional factor – its reputation for on-time delivery. In the wholesale meat market during the Asian bird flu epidemic in Spring 2004, chicken with a proven European source commanded a price premium based on health security – the product came with an emotional association of reassurance.

Often customers claim that the most important criterion is a lower price. The low-price myth is sustained by face-value research studies where customers, asked about acceptable price levels, always fish for a better deal. However, psychologists suggest that in these responses they may be hoping to influence the research sponsor to bring prices down. The importance of a low price can be exaggerated in purchase decisions. In fact, emotional associations often count for more than is admitted.

## Commanding a premium price – how Nike do it

**In the 1960s,** Phil Knight, founder of Nike, took the Stanford MBA programme. This programme featured a project, supervised by Frank Shallenberger, to design a small business including a marketing plan. Knight, a running enthusiast, was influenced by his coach, Bill Bowerman from the University of Oregon. Bowerman believed in superior running shoes. So unsurprisingly, Knight's business plan was to import high-quality/low-cost running shoes from Japan. In 1963, travelling through Japan on a world-tour, Knight called on a Japanese running shoe manufacturer: Tiger, a subsidiary of the Onitsuka company. On impulse, he gave his company name as Blue Ribbon Sports and soon after placed an order for Tigers. Working with Bowerman, he sold $8,000 worth of Tigers in his first year.

By 1971, sales had reached $1 million and Knight sought a name and a logo. Nike was the mythical Greek goddess of victory, symbolizing victorious encounters. For $35, advertising student, Caroline Davidson of Portland State University, designed a logo for him – the Swoosh symbol representing the wing of the goddess. During the 1970s, Nike became the company name. The company sponsored a runner called Steve Prefontaine and went on to sponsor other athletes. In 1985 sponsorship went to a young basketball player called Michael Jordan and the company developed Air Jordan basketball shoes. The range now covered other sports and Nike extended its range from sports clothing to street clothing. The 'Just do it' slogan appeared in 1988.

In 40 years, Nike has grown from two people in one country with a revenue of $8,000 to 23,000 Nike employees serving 120 countries and revenue for the financial year 2004 reaching $12.25 billion at a 42.9 percent gross margin. That is value creation.

## What did they get right?

The core of success was the development of a performance sports shoe. To a runner the most important goal is winning the race. Beating a closely matched rival requires absolute efficiency in muscle use. Nike shoes, with a waffle sole, were lighter than rival products and hence less muscle was required to lift the shoe and more power could be applied to velocity. Lighter shoes delivered faster times – just a hundredth of a second is sufficient to breast the tape first. Nike has worked with athletes from the beginning to innovate in sports shoes, apparel and equipment that help them to perform at the highest level. Nike creates value for the runner.

The adoption by athletes of Nike, symbolized by their wearing the Swoosh, has led to Nike becoming a street brand worn by athletes, aspiring athletes and, as Bill Bowerman said, 'if you have a body, you are an athlete'. It is a compelling image for many ambitious young and youthful people around the world. The benefit is the mental imagery – when they don Nike branded clothing associated with sports winners, they gain a sense of superiority. Nike creates value for the kid on the street.

Nike capture this value in a premium price: Nike Airmax 95 trainers are listed at £80 on www.kelkoo.co.uk, a leader in price comparison websites. The same site offers branded trainers at below £30. The man in the street knows that Nike trainers are sourced from the Far East and may even has seen an anti-Nike website quoting labour costs for Vietnam at $1.60 per day. They know that the manufacturing cost of the shoes is a fraction of the retail price, and yet they (or their parents) willingly pay a premium for the combination of tangible performance and intangible emotional connotations.

*Source*: www.nike.com and industry commentators.

In reality, customers talk about low prices, but truly they seek value. A higher price is acceptable when higher benefits are received. A lower price is expected when lower benefits are provided. This can be shown graphically. First, determine a scoring system for product benefits. For example, this might be power output for an electric motor, resale price after three years for a car, taste profile for margarine or a weighted index of a number of factors. The horizontal axis represents the score for product benefits. The price scale is shown on the vertical axis. Marking each product on this graph with benefit scores and price normally illustrates a 'value equivalence line' (see Figure 2.1). Higher on the line means higher price and higher benefits.

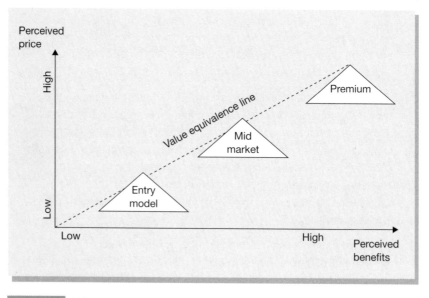

**Value equivalence line**

In markets where competitor shares are stable, rival products will be placed at various points along the value equivalence line. If a competitor moves off the line to offer superior value, you could expect customers to respond and for market share to grow. Superior value might be offered either by raising benefits or by lowering price. In the UK market for menswear, Next has offered higher perceived benefits of classical style and share has grown from 6.9 percent in 2001 to 7.3 percent in 2004 (see Table 2.1). The supermarket Asda has offered its 'George' brand at relatively low prices and seen share grow from 2.1 percent in 2001 to 3.8 percent in 2004.

Customers may not be spread evenly along the value equivalence line. Many markets show the 'hole in the middle' effect. You will find a large number of customers seeking lower specifications at an accessible price. Another cluster of customers look for the reassurance of higher standards at a more exclusive price level. For example, there is demand for four-star hotel accommodation with luxury and service as the motivation, and demand for two-star budget hotels. There are relatively few buyers in the middle market. We will look more at value segmentation in Chapter 4.

| Table 2.1 | Market share by value in the UK menswear market | | | |
|---|---|---|---|---|
| | *2004* | *2003* | *2002* | *2001* |
| Next | 7.2% | 7.1% | 7.0% | 6.9% |
| Asda | 3.8% | 3.2% | 2.8% | 2.1% |

*Source*: Mintel, quoted in *Marketing Magazine*, 2 March 2005.

# The tipping point of value

Brands create value for customers by developing products and services that customers need, and surrounding them with positive associations. Value can be defined as a combination of a set of product benefits plus emotional associations at an identified price level. See Figure 2.2.

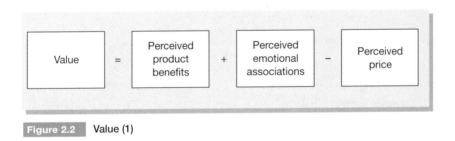

| Figure 2.2 | Value (1)

The right price is the tipping point where the benefits outweigh the customer's desire to keep money in their pocket. Smarter pricing means leveraging the value in the mind of the customer. The value equation provides six potential ways that superior value can be created in the mind of the customer:

**1 Raising the actual product (or service) benefits**

Product, service and packaging innovations come in this category. For example, a juice brand could improve the product with an easy-pour spout that is leak proof and re-sealable.

## 2  Raising the customer's perceptions of the product benefits

The skill here is to uncover clues from customer insights to convey quality subliminally. For example, the scent of lemon or pine is a low-cost addition to industrial cleaning fluids that raises the customer's perception of their efficacy. High specification instrumentation can imply that the machinery is high quality. The play quality of a DVD player is judged by the smoothness of the disc ejection system.

## 3  Building emotional associations

Consumer brands deliberately create emotional associations. Champagne is linked to celebration, the chocolate bar Kit-Kat is associated with taking a break from work. Industrial brands are now building particular associations. For example Caterpillar – the Illinois-based leader in machines, engines and construction equipment – focuses on providing confidence to meet contract deadlines. Companies are selecting relevant values and developing strategies to make them evident to customers. Examples are: flexibility, easy-to-do-business with or professionalism.

## 4  Increasing awareness of the emotional aspects

The challenge is to find creative ways to remind customers of positive emotional benefits. Typically rail travellers notice a train's timing only when it is running late – most train operating companies make apologetic announcements drawing attention to lateness. First Great Western Train Managers *also* make announcements alerting customers to on-time arrivals, as they thank people for travelling with them. Ensure customers notice quality, reliability, performance and consistency, lest they simply take your virtues for granted.

## 5  Lowering the actual price

Sometimes there are good commercial reasons to lower prices. However, you should cut prices only in return for a reciprocal benefit. Examples are greater volume, greater security, longer commitment, agreeing to share data or to co-develop a new opportunity. Smarter pricing does not give away margin in return for nothing.

### 6  Lowering the perceived price

The actual price is not as critical as the perceptions of price. It is possible to alter price perceptions without reducing prices. For example, men are often brief on telephone landlines believing that phone calls are 'expensive'. The UK phone company, BT, has tried to address this price perception with advertising that compares the cost of a phone call favourably with the price of a pint of beer. Other companies express the cost of insurance in terms of cost per day covered rather than giving the big number of an annual premium.

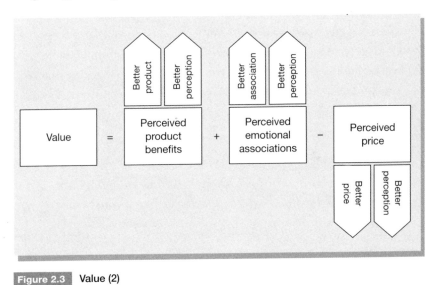

**Figure 2.3**    Value (2)

# The value proposition

Success comes from offering specific customers a clear combination of benefit and price that they will find attractive. A statement summarizing this targeted offer is called a 'value proposition'. Its purpose is to unify the internal efforts to focus everyone on delivering a value package.

Returning to the Nike example at the beginning of this chapter, an illustration of their possible value proposition follows:

- **Precise benefits:** a sense of superiority from performance sports shoes associated with winners.

- **To which group?:** ambitious, youthful people around the world.

- **At what price?:** 300 percent premium over basic athletic shoes.

Nike's value proposition has identified the specific values that its customers seek. The company then designs a stream of products, product enhancements and brand communications that deliver this package. The author knows of no market in the world where Nike acts out of line with the broad direction of the above value proposition. In essence, the value proposition is a concise internal statement of the precise benefits offered to a specified target group at a defined price.

Business markets similarly need value propositions that encapsulate their offers to their customers. The offers include the intangible benefits of peace of mind for the sender or recipient of the package. For example, a value proposition for DHL might read as follows:

- **Precise benefits:** peace of mind through traceable reliable world-wide 24-hour package delivery.

- **To which group?:** international companies requiring time-sensitive deliveries.

- **At what price?:** 25 percent premium price (estimate).

Again DHL's customer activities are aligned by a single concept of 'what good looks like'.

The value proposition is about making choices. It is neither possible, nor credible to own all the virtues. You cannot be newest and most proven, nor the highest quality and the lowest price, nor the simplest and the most flexible. A single value proposition cannot appeal to all customers.

# The target group: what does it need? What can it afford?

The value proposition includes a clear target group. Understanding this group is important. One particular question is crucial – what can it afford? Smarter pricing must take into account what purchasers in this group are able to pay for a product or service and design products accordingly.

The most successful car launch of all time began with a specific group of people in mind – 15 to 24-year-olds in 1960s USA, a group growing by 11.5 million during the decade, with a higher proportion destined to go to college and earn enough to buy a new car. Market research highlighted their problem – their ideal car was not available. They were eager to own a car that looked expensive, stylish and sporty with bucket seats but would seat four people. And the maximum amount they could afford to pay was $2,500. With this target value proposition in mind, Lee Iacocca's design team developed the Ford Mustang. The price constraint was met by adapting Ford Falcon components under a new body-shell with a long sleek hood and a short deck. Of course it featured front bucket seats. In a nutshell, they produced a 'poor man's Thunderbird for the working girl', launching it on 14 April 1964 at the New York World's Fair. It was priced at $2,368, not much more than the 1960s Volkswagen Beetle.

The result – 22,000 orders were placed on the first day and 418,000 models were sold in the first 12 months – a record never subsequently matched. As Iacocca put it, 'when the product is right, you don't need to be a great marketer'. Success came from designing and making affordable exactly what the buyers wanted.

Similarly, Vodafone targeted a particular group with a new value proposition for mobile phones. Inhibited by techno-complexity, older people had resisted the appeal of mobile telephony. So, in May 2005, Vodafone Simply was launched in the UK, Spain and Portugal. The stripped down phones have just three functions: to make phone calls, send and receive text messages. They are operated by three large and straightforward dedicated buttons. Taking away a dozen technological features has created value for older non-users of mobile phones who are bamboozled by digital complexity.

# Dynamic propositions and value innovation

Finally, nothing stays the same. The value proposition cannot remain static. It must flex and change with the needs, expectations and choices available to the customer.

The value proposition of the *Financial Times* in 1990 would have included the precise benefit of being the primary trusted source of share price data and business news. As Michael Skapinker pointed out, today on-line share data are freely available. The *FT* decided that, as people could get their news for free, it would have to sell more analysis, comment and interviews with business leaders as an improved value proposition.

Value innovation may mean adding new features and services. It is good to provide levels of service that have not been offered in the market previously. For example, IKEA offer immediate availability for large items of furnishing while other stores quote weeks for delivery. However, it is important to remember the affordability factor. IKEA also remove other benefits that customers value less highly – stores are located out of city centre shopping areas and items must be self-assembled. Value innovation involves removing as well as adding features and benefits. The concept of value innovation is explored by W. Chan Kim and Renée Mauborgne. Their message is that it pays to challenge the conventional parameters. Do not accept industry conditions as a given.

Build the customer's perception and you can command higher prices. Keep the momentum by adding to that perception with value innovation.

# Chapter summary

- Despite claims that price is the most important factor, customers actually seek value. This comes from a combination of product (or service) performance plus an emotional association.

- Higher perceived benefits will justify a higher price on a value equivalence line. There are six potential ways to build perceptions of superior value in the mind of the customer.

- The value proposition defines the package of benefits and price for a target customer group.

- Focus on the target group. What does it need? What can it afford? Answering these questions can generate opportunities for value innovation.

- Markets, customers and competitors move on and value propositions must be updated.

# Management questions for your business

- Where do customers cluster on the value equivalence line for our industry?

- Do we have evidence of the price perceptions held by our customers? What shapes these perceptions and how might we influence them?

- What is our value proposition for each segment served?

- How could we innovate to deliver value to segments constrained by affordability?

- How has our value proposition responded to market, customer and competitor changes?

# Going further – references and additional reading

Bainbridge, J. (2005) 'Dressed for success' with Mintel data, *Marketing Magazine*, 3 March.

Kim, W. C. and Mauborgne, R. (1997) 'Value innovation the strategic logic of high growth', *Harvard Business Review*, January/February.

Lanning, M. J. (1998) *Delivering Profitable Value: A Revolutionary Framework to Accelerate Growth, Generate Wealth, and Rediscover the Heart of Business*, Capstone, Oxford.

Marn, M., Roegner, E. V. and Zawada, C. C. (2004), *The Price Advantage*, Wiley, Hoboken, NJ – see particularly Chapter 4, 'Product market strategy on value mapping'.

Nagle, T. and Holden, R. K. (2002) *Strategy and Tactics of Pricing*, Prentice Hall, Upper Saddle River, NJ.

Skapinker, M. (2004) 'The world's relentless march makes for hard times', *Financial Times*, 19 May.

www.dhl.com

www.kelkoo.co.uk for price comparisons.

www.nike.com for information about the Nike brand.

# 3

# What would you pay for this? Perils and pitfalls of pricing research

*The customer entered the car showroom and admired the metallic black coupé by the window. The professional car salesman came over and opened a conversation. He asked a lot of questions. The one question he never asked was 'how much would you pay for this model?' He needed the answer to do the deal but an oblique approach was needed.*

*Where do you work, what kind of job do you have? (Indicates what he or she can afford.)*

*Questions about family and holidays uncover willingness to spend money and priorities.*

*Questions about other models being considered illustrates knowledge of the market place and market prices.*

*Where do you live? (Discovers the convenience of the dealer's location and therefore the value to the buyer.)*

*By the end of the conversation, the salesman knows the level of deal needed to win the sale. He has researched the customer's ability and willingness to pay, his or her needs, and knowledge of competitors and the value of the vehicle, without ever sensitizing the customer to price.*

There are three basic approaches to price-setting. See Figure 3.1.

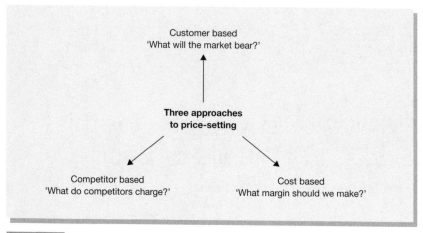

Customer based
'What will the market bear?'

**Three approaches
to price-setting**

Competitor based
'What do competitors charge?'

Cost based
'What margin should we make?'

**Figure 3.1**    Approaches to price-setting

## 1   Mark-up pricing

The first method is to look at costs and mark-up an acceptable margin. This may be used as a rule of thumb, for example by an industrial wholesaler who obtains numerous items from different sources. Mark-up is a short-cut to making hundreds of pricing decisions that ensure all products are contributing to profitability. Tools are available for mark-up pricing: see an example on the website of Santa Cruz-based Steiner Marketing www.steinermarketing.com/calc_markup_pricing.htm

However, costs are an internal matter and cost-based prices are unlikely to capture an appropriate share of the potential value of the market place. Look at the margins achieved by popcorn vendors and balloon sellers. They do not base retail prices on the cost of the raw materials.

## 2   Follow the competitor

The second method is to study competitors. In this situation, companies set prices primarily by reference to one or more other players in the market. For instance, 500 airlines (with the notable exception of Southwest Airlines) participate in a fare publishing enterprise called the Airline Tariff Publishing Company (ATPCO) founded in 1965 and now owned jointly by 19 leading airlines.

ATPCO collects fares (and rules such as refundability) and publishes these back to the airlines and reservation services. A major airline may have over a million prices in the market place with 10–20 prices per flight, hundreds of destinations and variation by day of the week and month. Fare changes may be notified three times each weekday and once a day at weekends. Each competitor knows all the prices that every other competitor offers and learns of any changes within hours. According to Charles Fishman, writing in *Fast Company* (2003), if one carrier cuts a price, there could be 400,000 price changes with rivals following suite. Sophisticated computer technology allows airlines to spiral down to break-even points or even losses. This ongoing reactive approach treats products and services as commodities. It assumes that your goods are identical to competitors, with price as the only basis for choice. It disregards differentiation and ignores the value created for the buyer.

## 3  What the market will bear

The third method is to see what the market will bear. This approach identifies what the customer is willing to pay for the item. eBay is a pure example of a way in which a seller can assess how much a customer values a product. Prospective buyers see descriptions and illustrations of products and then bid competitively until the auction closes. This method comes closer to capturing full value because the person bidding the most for the item is successful. The more competitive the bidding, the more effective is the value capture.

But most companies serving large numbers of customers in complex markets with ranges of products will be unable to auction every item. So how might you discover what the market will bear? How do you ensure that items or services are not under-priced, leaving value on the table? The customer will not tell you that he or she was prepared to pay more. So a way to discover the answer is through pricing analysis and research.

# Serious price research – done by the few

Surprisingly few companies use pricing research effectively. A survey quoted by Kent B. Monroe and Jennifer L. Cox, writing in *Marketing Management* (September 2001), found that 88 percent of companies did little or no serious pricing research. Only 8 percent of companies could be classified as professionally conducting pricing research to support the development of an effective pricing strategy. This is corroborated by a McKinsey & Company pricing benchmark study that estimated only about 15 percent of companies do serious price research.

See Table 3.1 for a summary of the available tools, techniques and approaches:

| Table 3.1 | Pricing research and analysis |
|---|---|
| Intention-based | Direct questioning |
| | Gabor–Granger buy response question |
| | price sensitivity meter (PSM) |
| | Conjoint analysis |
| | Discrete choice modelling (DCM) |
| Purchase-based | Historical sales data |
| | Panel data |
| | Store scanner data |
| | Purchase laboratory experiments |
| | In-store experiments |

## Intention-based research

Some companies use pricing research to uncover buyers' intentions. They endeavour to gather meaningful customer input in a competitive context. Customer research on prices is notoriously difficult to interpret and sometimes unreliable.

According to Baker, Marn and Zawada (2001) writing on the subject of setting Internet prices, customers claim to buy on-line for the lower prices. Yet their behaviour tells a different story. McKinsey & Company research showed that 89 percent of on-line book buyers bought from the first site visited. Similarly with 84 percent of toy buyers and 81 percent of music buyers. Fewer than 10 percent of Internet purchasers – according to a separate survey – turned out to be deliberate bargain hunters. Customers say one thing and do another.

## Direct questioning

Customers seem unable to answer honestly the question: how much would you pay for this? David W. Lyon's award-winning article 'The price is right (or is it?)' (2002), states the obvious problem with this question: 'Hearing such a question, many respondents immediately shift into bargaining mode and produce opening offers that aren't even remotely reflective of what their real world behaviour would be.' Customers may hope to encourage price cuts or simply be unable to admit to intangible reasons for paying more than a minimum. It is unwise to develop a strategy based on reactions to customers leveraging one supplier over another to get the best possible price.

## Buy response question

A simple but more reliable direct question is the 'buy response question'. Known as the Gabor–Granger technique after the economists who invented it in the 1960s, the method is to describe or demonstrate a product with its features, mentioning the price in context. The customer is asked, 'Would you buy it?' The price should be presented unobtrusively, so it is seen as just one of the features of the product. It is important that the respondent's attention is not drawn specifically to the price tag. It is also possible to present a range of competitor products and to pose the question 'which, if any, would you buy?'

To gauge price sensitivity, it is essential to test different price options. Obviously, if a single respondent were presented with a second option – a package identical apart from a price change – then he or she will be sensitized to price and revert to bargaining mode. Sequential tests may be appealing in terms of reducing research costs, but they actually destroy meaning. Therefore monadic tests are used – each respondent is asked once only. Prices vary between different respondents in the overall sample. Respondents are unaware that others are being shown different prices or that price is the object of the survey. Gabor–Granger tests are simple, defensible and widely used to predict demand at different price levels – sometimes called purchase probability curves. These can be used to forecast optimum revenue. Unless the offering is priced so low that the customer questions its quality, you would expect the lowest price to result in the highest share.

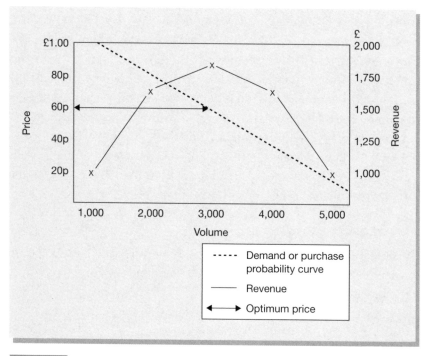

Figure 3.2    Gabor–Granger price volume curve

The key limitation of this test is that accuracy is a function of the sample size. For each price step, a sample size of more than 200 is required in order to give a reasonable level of confidence. Where price changes are as small as 5–10 percent, larger than normal sample sizes are needed for statistical accuracy. According to David W. Lyon, cell sizes of less than 100 are not uncommon in leading to large sampling errors – even paradoxical reversals of the expected price–volume relationship. Recommended techniques to increase accuracy include the use of larger samples, a smaller number of price steps tested and bigger differences between the chosen prices.

*Price sensitivity meter*

There is a more sophisticated version of the Gabor–Granger technique, devised by the Dutch psychologist Peter van Westendorp in the 1970s. This is most often used for new products where there is no obvious value benchmark or competitor equivalent. The van Westendorp Price Sensitivity Meter (PSM) describes or demonstrates the product as before and then poses four questions:

- At what price would you consider this product to represent good value?
- At what price would you say this item is getting expensive but you would still consider buying it?
- At what price would you consider this product to be too expensive to consider buying it?
- At what price would you consider this product to be priced so cheaply that you would worry about quality?

There is an intersection point where the number of respondents who regard the product as too expensive exactly equals the number who see it as too cheap. This intersection is the recommended price and the other questions hopefully illuminate the likely acceptable range of prices.

However, according to David W. Lyon, many PSM respondents give figures that are internally inconsistent. In fact, despite the intuitive appeal of the four questions, they are simply variants of the 'How much would you pay for this?' question and therefore risk the bias mentioned above. As such, this technique is best reserved for exploring potential prices on highly innovative products. Conclusions should be tested with other studies such as the monadic method or trade-off analysis.

*Conjoint analysis*

Trade-off or conjoint analysis is a statistical technique developed by Luce, a mathematical psychologist, and Tukey, a statistician. It reflects the reality of how the human brain makes decisions. The technique compels respondents to make 'either/or' choices that effectively rank benefits and benefit combinations against different price points. An example is the trade-off customers make to buy fuel on their route home from work. How much lower must the fuel on the other side of the road be priced in order to compensate for the inconvenience of crossing the carriageway?

Respondents are invited to chose between different paired offers (see Figure 3.3). The offers consist of various attributes and for each attribute a number of levels. For example, one attribute of a laptop computer might be portability and the levels might be three specified weights. Another attribute might be processing speed with three levels, and similarly for style and price. Each offer pairs a higher level of one attribute and a lower level of another at different price points.

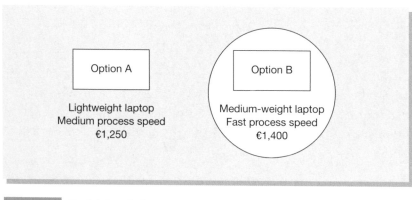

Option A

Lightweight laptop
Medium process speed
€1,250

Option B

Medium-weight laptop
Fast process speed
€1,400

Figure 3.3    Conjoint analysis

By giving a significant number of choices to a representative sample, which should be in excess of 200 for statistical significance, it is possible to develop a robust model of the price people are prepared to pay for potential combinations of benefits. Customers' preferences for different offers are ranked and then decomposed in order to determine each person's inferred 'utility function' or value for each element of the benefit package. Respondents' choices show the trade-offs they would make and convey the relative importance of each attribute in numerical terms.

Conjoint analysis can be administered cost effectively on-line, for instance once the sample has been qualified by telephone recruitment. The expanding Bath-based market research agency, Dobney, has devised a simple illustration of how an on-line conjoint analysis can refine the understanding of priorities, see 'Conjoint analysis in action' on the website www.dobney.com

In *Marketing Management*, Philip Kotler cites how the mid-market hotel brand, Courtyard by Marriott, developed its value proposition through the use of conjoint analysis – determining appealing and profitable benefit combinations.

There is a recognized bias in conjoint analysis: it tends to imply lower price sensitivity than occurs in reality. Perhaps hypothetical product images on screen accompanied by a list of features in words are insufficient and, in this context, the price begins to act as a subliminal indicator of likely quality in use. People may subconsciously assume that the higher priced product is somehow better – the concept of 'you get what you pay for' – which will skew their responses in a way that would not be reflected if they were comparing products physically in store.

Conjoint analysis has the opposite shortcomings when non-price factors are significant and price itself is less important in the real-world decision. For example, in a safety related market where brand reputation is critical, the artificiality of conjoint analysis may imply greater price sensitivity than is the case in reality. In the pharmaceuticals market, doctors tend to be more concerned with clinical effectiveness and limited side effects than price, but this may not be reflected in conjoint studies.

Focus groups are an important way of identifying the attributes that would be used in conjoint analysis. They may also suggest the options and levels that need to be selected. However, the group dynamics and influence factors mean that reactions to prices in focus groups may be misleading.

In-depth interviews with individual consumers or customers can help draw out how users perceive the product and its value to them in use. These interviews will be useful to discover which are the critical product benefits. Particularly in a business-to-business context, reseachers may infer the monetary value of a product or service – how it supports revenue earning for the customer or cuts their costs – without asking the direct question. In-depth interviews are especially relevant in teasing out psychological or emotional benefits that a customer considers significant.

### Discrete choice modelling

Discrete Choice Modelling (DCM) is a refinement of conjoint analysis, where the offers are presented as competing products from named brands with elaborated specifications and performance details described. Ideally, respondents are able to examine and handle sample products. This addresses the 'hypothetical' concern with conjoint analysis.

Typically, three competing brands would be offered instead of the paired trade-off, and specifications and benefits would mirror the market situation. Once the product options are clearly understood the respondents select one of the three priced packages shown on screen. At this point the DCM software generates a slightly different set of choices, perhaps with a longer warranty for one brand. The respondent chooses from the new set. If the choice has remained the same, the software creates another option, perhaps lowering a price of one of the other brands. If the choice has now changed the software tests this new choice with further variants. Overall maybe 12 to 15 choices would be made. Taken as a whole, these choices contribute to a better understanding of the value map and may indicate opportunities to increase prices or raise specifications to command a higher price in the market.

It might be imagined that DCM would show a higher sensitivity to price since it is evidently about price. This is not borne out in practice and the reason may be linked to the fact that very specific products are presented in a context mirroring reality.

# Perils of price questions

Probing intentions and preferences around price has perils. All the approaches and techniques mentioned carry with them the risk that predicted behaviour may not occur in practice. Any survey about price holds dangers that people will not be able to reflect their normal behaviour in an artificial environment. They may exaggerate the importance of price when the researcher focuses his or her attention on this element, or may be distracted by numerous appealing features, so that the role that price has in making real decisions is underplayed.

For this reason the most reliable findings come when real people are making normal decisions in a familiar environment. If it is possible to use actual behaviour as the guide then do so.

## Purchase-based data

### Historical sales data

Internal records of sales are normally readily available. Many organizations have comprehensive records of purchases by individual customers from which responses to price increases or promotional discounts may be deduced. The costs of computer processing, data inference and modelling are falling, and software packages are available to help. Modelling buyer behaviour following price increases can lead to conclusions about the timing of price hikes. For example, where products or services are clearly seasonal, annual price increases can be moved to the start of the peak selling period in order to stimulate sales in the slack period and capture value as demand rises.

Care is needed in interpretation. For example, sales to wholesalers or intermediaries may include inventory fluctuations and fail to reflect end-user patterns. Trends may relate to non-price factors. These may be responses to external occurrences, such as unusual weather patterns or political, economic or religious events. Analyzing sales of chocolate among Christian users may show unusual patterns around Lent – when buyers forego pleasures in the run-up to Easter. Easter is a festival whose calendar timing varies according to the phases of the moon. Ramadan is another lunar festival whose timing varies from year to year, which may skew year-on-year trend data.

Market factors may also distort results and make interpretation problematic. Examples of disruptive market events are:

- New product launches and customer anticipation of future launches.
- Changes in advertising weights or campaign messages by the brand studied or by competitor brands.
- Product promotions by the brand studied or competitor brands.
- Stock shortages or delivery problems by competitors.

Retail sales data covering major brands bought from research organizations, such as AC Nielsen, can allow some of these factors to be taken into account. However, historical sales reflect a plethora of influences on purchase behaviour and price is only one of these factors. It may not be possible to take out the extraneous effects.

### Panel data

In consumer markets with multiple products and frequent transactions, panels of buyers provide solid data. A number of research agencies recruit and maintain consumer panels whose members record their actual purchases. For example, the AC Nielsen Worldwide Consumer Panel Services cover 18 countries around the world, capturing actual consumer purchase information for almost 125,000 households. This purchase information shows the actual items bought, price paid and any coupons used or discounts taken. Market share changes can be tracked against relative prices of competing brands. Subject to sample size, it is also possible to correlate price sensitivity with consumer demographics.

Of course the quality of the data depends on how accurately the panel represents the market. Recruiting typical consumers may not be easy, because those joining panels may simply be more interested in shopping, product comparisons and prices than the overall market. Time-scarce buyers are less price-sensitive – they don't have time to make price comparisons. By their very nature, panels may tend to attract time-rich consumers. This drawback is being reduced by newer techniques that simplify obligations of panel membership. No longer do consumers need to keep purchase diaries. Technology allows consumers to buy with a special credit card or have their purchases scanned in store.

## Store scanner data

Some grocery retailers will also sell or make available to manufacturers the results from store scanners. Sometimes this information will be provided to a 'category captain' or lead brand that is required to evaluate the price and product performance of all brands and then impartially recommend to the retailer changes to brands, packs or pricing that can grow the overall category.

## Purchase laboratory experiments

This technique is used to investigate what the market will bear. For a business-to-business example let us look at DHL, the global air express transportation company. Writing in *Fast Company*, Charles Fishman (2003) describes the research conducted for DHL by the Texas-based pricing consultancy Zilliant. Its skill is to measure what the market will bear. Rather than trying to get the price right mathematically, Zilliant will *look* for the right price. They don't raise prices across the board by 5 percent and watch for customer defection, nor cut prices by 15 percent and hope for a 20 percent sales increase. Instead, the software runs numerous experiments, testing slightly changed prices on real customers. They test a new price in a controlled way, measuring the response of cells of customers. Tests covered prices for all weights of package across 43 different markets. There were thousands of data points. Specifically, the software measured customers who called, asked for a price and then did not ship – failed prices. These failed prices indicated the price ceiling. Lower prices calibrated the potential for volume increase. The results showed that DHL – with its strong international reputation – did not need to match lower-priced rivals UPS and FedEx. Hundreds of prices were changed. Some prices were lowered slightly, still maintaining a premium over competitors, while gaining volume, revenue and profit.

The ratio of customers who check for a price and then fail to buy is a valid measure of pricing effectiveness used by smarter Internet businesses. Software can track the number of customers who view a product or investigate specifications on-screen and also measure the proportion of these who proceed to book an order. If the 'look to book' ratio rises then prices may be too high. More importantly, if all those who look, also proceed to book orders, then the price may be too low.

### In-store experiments

Retailers are able to test different prices and price relationships in different stores to determine the levels that optimize sales, or revenue, or profitability. Eleven million customers of Tesco – the UK-based supermarket – hold 'Clubcards'. This is a customer reward mechanism that permits the company to monitor every single purchase these customers make in store. With this tracking system, Tesco can test new prices on real customers and measure responses precisely. In this way, they use collective customer responses to point to the right price.

## Pricing research – the bottom line

The conclusion to draw is that price research is fraught with perils of exaggeration and under-estimation. Respondents find it almost impossible to be dispassionate about prices. Expert advice from pricing consultancies is necessary. A good place to start is the Professional Pricing Society. You must still be mindful that research on intentions is only a support or challenge to executive judgement. The best test of what customers will pay is to run live experiments and monitor the results closely.

Testing what the market will bear is a better way to capture full value than mark-up pricing or following competitors' price lists.

## Chapter summary

- There are three approaches to pricing:
  - basing prices on costs
  - following the competitor
  - establishing what the market will bear.

▦ Finding out what the market will bear is critical to ensure that products and services are not under-priced and that value is not left on the table. One way of testing what the market will bear is through auctions. For most businesses, interpreting historical sales data and undertaking pricing research are more practical approaches.

▦ Customers are often unable to answer honestly the question: 'How much would you pay for this?' Consequently, pricing research is designed to deflect attention away from the price itself. Rather, it attempts to discern the customer's perception of value. There are techniques such as the Gabor–Granger 'buy response question' and the van Westendorp 'price sensitivity meter'.

▦ Alternatively, you can draw conclusions by inviting customers to trade-off one benefit against others in a conjoint analysis or through discrete choice modelling.

▦ All questions around preferences and intentions carry risks that real-life behaviour will differ. Thus, wherever possible, it is better to use actual purchase behaviour to test price ceilings and optimal price levels.

## Management questions for your business

▦ Are we leaving value on the table? Are some of our products and services under-priced?

▦ Are price perceptions gauged analytically with statistically significant samples, or are general perceptions extrapolated from the views of a small number of vocal customers or sales people?

▦ Would conjoint analysis help price new lines more judiciously?

▦ How could we test new prices on real customers?

# Going further – references and additional reading

Baker, W., Marn, M. and Zawada, C. C. (2001) 'Price smarter on the net', *Harvard Business Review*, February.

Feldman, D. (2002) 'The pricing puzzle', *Marketing Research*, Winter.

Fishman, C. (2003) 'Which price is right', *Fast Company*, March.

Green, P., Carroll, J. and Goldberg, S. (1981) 'A general approach to product design optimization via conjoint analysis', *Journal of Marketing*, 43.

Green, P. and Srinivasan, V. (1978) 'Conjoint analysis in consumer research: issues and outlook', *Journal of Consumer Research*, 5.

Kotler. P. (2003) *Marketing Management* 11th edition, Prentice Hall, Upper Saddle River, NJ.

Lyon, D. W. (2002) 'The price is right (or is it?)', *Marketing Research*, Winter.

Marn, M., Roegner, E. V. and Zawada, C. C. (2004) *The Price Advantage*, Wiley Finance, see especially Chapter 14.

Monroe, K. and Cox, J. (2001) 'Pricing practices that endanger profits', *Marketing Magazine*, September/October.

Nagle, T. and Holden, R. K. (2002) *The Strategy and Tactics of Pricing*, Prentice Hall, Upper Saddle River, NJ, see Chapter 13 'Measuring perceived value and price sensitivity'.

www.dobney.com for on-line conjoint analysis example.

www.pricingsociety.com – Professional Pricing Society website.

www.zilliant.com for pricing research.

# 4

# Price discrimination – segmenting by price sensitivity

### How Glaxo turned price sensitivity into benefit promise

**When pharmaceutical company Glaxo** launched their anti-ulcer treatment, 'Zantac', in 1983, they had to price against an established incumbent brand sold by SmithKline. This brand was 'Tagamet', then the world's biggest selling drug. The obvious options were to enter with a parallel price or to undercut the dominant brand. The obvious options were wrong. At the same or lower price the market would see Zantac as a me-too equivalent with no reason to change.

Glaxo knew that Zantac required only twice daily dosage instead of Tagamet's four times per day regime. It also offered fewer side effects. Understanding the price sensitivity of their market, Glaxo priced Zantac at an astonishing 50 percent premium over Tagamet. The higher price drew attention to the differentiation. It challenged physicians to consider Zantac. Physicians judged that it must be the more potent drug. Zantac sales soared past Tagamet and Glaxo's profits increased in five years from around £90 million per year to over £600 million.

Capturing value means establishing the ceiling price acceptable to customers and the optimal price that yields the most profitable combination of volume and price. Management judgement supported by research tries to calibrate the price–volume relationship. Understanding how sensitive customers are to prices is essential in order to achieve higher prices

# Price–volume relationship

When a price rises, fewer people are able or willing to buy and the remaining buyers may decrease their purchasing quantity or frequency. Higher tax on cigarettes raises prices to discourage smoking. When prices fall more buyers enter the market and purchase occasions rise. As the price of DVD players has fallen, more and more households have bought them.

Economists call this relationship the price elasticity of demand:

$$E = \frac{\text{\% change in unit sales}}{\text{\% change in price}}$$

This measures the percentage change in a product's unit sales as a result of a change in price. The demand elasticity, $E$ is normally a negative number because positive price changes (or increases) usually result in sales declines.

There is a figure for market elasticity – the price level offered by the market as a whole will impact on total purchase volumes. There is also a cross-elasticity between the players in a market, where a price reduction or increase by one supplier will have an impact on sales relative to competitors. Generally brands with larger shares will show lower cross-elasticity through the loyalty of their customers.

Researchers Bijmolt, van Heerde and Pieters conducted a meta-analysis of 1,851 price elasticities drawn from 81 previous studies. They calculated that the average price elasticity is –2.62. They discovered that, compared with a previous meta-analysis, price elasticity had increased. In effect, consumers have become more price-sensitive. The researchers comment on this deal-making behaviour and suggest that a way to avoid this may be to reduce the frequency of price promotions.

Other conclusions from this meta-analysis are that consumers are more price-elastic for durables than for other goods. They found that consumer demand for products is considerably more price-elastic in the introduction and growth phases of the life-cycle than in maturity.

# Buying *more* as the price rises!

There are exceptions and limits to price elasticity when prices reach levels implying either unbelievably high or unacceptably low standards of performance. For example, few parents would buy a child's car safety seat priced 60 percent lower than competing products because it breaches the zone of credibility. There are also a small number of examples of positive values for $E$, typically in status-related products. Research by Angela Chao and Juliet B. Schor in 1998 found that demand for cosmetics, such as lipstick, eye-shadow and mascara, among college-educated women *increased* as the price rose. The price coefficient was +0.117. In a broader sample of females the coefficient was found to be conventionally negative (–0.157).

The higher the value for $E$, the more elastic is the demand and the greater will be the sales response as a result of price changes.

**Action:** how to gain from price indifference bands

The practical aspects of price elasticity have been investigated in research by McKinsey & Company. The consulting firm has identified 'pricing indifference bands' – a range of possible prices within which price changes have little or no impact on customer purchase decisions. These bands may range as wide as 17 percentage points for branded consumer beauty products and as narrow as 0.2 percent in certain financial products. Placing a product higher within the indifference band will make a significant profit difference.

Figure 4.1 shows two products priced at exactly the same level. With an understanding of the indifference band for customers in this market, there is an opportunity for product A to raise its price to the top of the band and capture substantially greater value without any consequent loss in sales to product B. However, an increase beyond the indifference brand marked by the dotted line, will bring into play the normal levels of cross-elasticity.

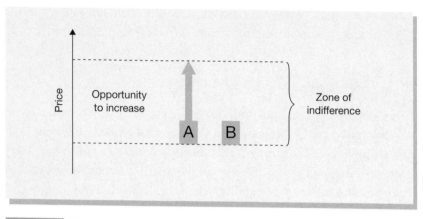

Zone of indifference

# Driving miles to buy cheap petrol

Price sensitivity of customers varies dramatically between different product categories and is not always logical. There is a curious phenomenon about petrol purchases investigated by Marcel Cohen (1999). He describes how purchasers will sometimes go considerably out of their way to hunt for the cheapest petrol, forfeiting much of the benefit that a cheaper price might provide by seeking it. Customers show an obsession with prices in this market despite the fact that the spread of prices is small with a range of less than 1 percent between the highest and lowest prices in a market. Even if a customer consistently bought the most expensive petrol, it would have little impact on his or her overall motoring costs which are dominated by depreciation in value, servicing and repairs. Cohen suggests that this is because petrol is seen as a necessity, vital for freedom of movement. The emotional perception that petrol companies have exploited this dependency at times of shortage has led to resentment which shows itself in price-hunting as a means to get back at the oil companies. In turn, oil companies have sensitized customers to price with large external displays of prices expressed in decimals of currency per litre.

Price sensitivity can vary over time. Innovative customers and early adopters tend to be less price-sensitive when they discover new and unique products. The first buyers of iPods paid a price premium. As markets mature, novelty fades and customers become more familiar with product characteristics. There is the danger that price becomes a greater factor in purchases. Retail advertisements and displays for mature products like refrigerators and ovens often highlight the price more than the benefits.

# Nine effects to reduce price sensitivity

Thomas Nagle and Reed K. Holden, writing in *The Strategy and Tactics of Pricing* (2002) identify nine 'effects' that influence willingness to pay and cause buyers to be more or less price sensitive to the difference between price and value (as listed in Table 4.1). A full account is given in Chapter 4 of their book.

**Table 4.1**    Nine effects to reduce price sensitivity

| | | |
|---|---|---|
| Reference price effect | Price-quality effect | Shared-cost effect |
| Difficult comparison effect | Expenditure effect | Fairness effect |
| Switching cost effect | End-benefit effect | Framing effect |

*Source*: Nagle and Holden (2002).

## 1   Reference price effect

Willingness to pay is influenced by the perceptions buyers have of the relative cost of an alternative. If customers are unaware of substitutes they will be less price-sensitive. If they are aware of an alternative they will use this as a benchmark. Memory of previous purchases will give an understanding of acceptable value. Where they see comparisons side by side in a retail store this will also encourage confidence in making a purchase and shape the resultant behaviour. The *Financial Times*, 31 January 2005, carried a report on Seiyu, the Japanese retailing affiliate of Wal-Mart. Seiyu admitted sales had been lost as a result of too narrow a product range. 'For example, we made the mistake of featuring only ¥197 packs of toilet paper, when we should also have featured packs for ¥450, so consumers can choose', said a Sieyu spokesman.

Vendors can help to set benchmarks. If sales people offer a higher-priced option initially, it encourages customers to be less price-sensitive over subsequent items they consider. The Hawkshead mail order catalogue for summer 2005 offers a range of hiking footwear – the first items are priced at £48 and £58, making the lower priced boots on the following pages seem to represent excellent value.

**Action:** Help customers for your products to notice reference prices that convey the true value you offer.

## 2   Difficult comparison effect

Willingness to pay is influenced by the ease of making valid comparisons. If the product or service alternative is difficult to evaluate, for example legal services, then customers will be less price-sensitive about buying from a trustworthy firm or brand.

Low-priced competitors will try to make the comparison easy for buyers by imitating the pack colours or design of the leading brand. Manufacturers design and trademark packs with non-standard shapes or unique quantities to make comparison more difficult. It is harder to compare when price becomes less obvious through separating taxes, surcharges, shipping and handling. Some conference organizers promote overseas events and quote prices in local currency to make comparison with home costs harder.

**Action:** Make the comparison with lower-priced products less obvious.

## 3   Switching cost effect

The greater the amount of switching costs, the less price-sensitive will be the customers. These costs may be directly financial:

- Extended credit
- Penalty contracts
- Cumulative terms
- Price guarantees
- Buy-back guarantee
- Forecasting service
- Managing inventory
- Proprietary systems

- Providing equipment
- Joint ventures
- Creating industry standards
- Ingredient brands
- Common catalogues
- Electronic links
- Reciprocal business
- Designing for customers
- Design for end-user
- Help-line for end-users
- Staff training
- Out-source service.

In addition there can be psychological switching costs:

- Service guarantees
- Satisfaction-based pricing
- Back-up resources
- Training and education
- Support to colleges/universities
- Information provision
- Brand image
- Quality awards
- Reputation for innovation
- Exceeding international standards
- Reminders of value
- User-group membership
- Access to facilities
- Website links
- Focus on risks
- Stories of switching disasters.

**Action:** Analyze and develop both categories of switching costs. Build barriers to exit which help to desensitize customers to price. Smart suppliers have a strategy to deliberately identify, construct and make customers aware of the difficulties, uncertainties and risks of changing supply source.

### 4  Price-quality effect

Prestige, signified by high price, counteracts price sensitivity. If you have to ask the price of a Ferrari then perhaps you cannot afford it. Halving the list price of a Rolex would make it much less effective in conveying to others the wealth of the owner. Some other products, wine for example, which are hard to judge unopened, may be bought using price as a signal of relative quality.

**Action:** Use clear price steps as a means of communicating increasing benefits through the range.

### 5  Expenditure effect

Buyers will naturally be more price-sensitive when the expenditure involved represents a significant portion of their available income. Higher spending means more focus on price. Thus a snack bought in isolation will be bought spontaneously, but the same snack bought as part of the weekly supermarket shop will be subject to closer scrutiny. It is therefore important for a vendor to understand the context and the significance of the spend to the buyer at the point of purchase.

**Action:** Look for buying occasions when the price is less critical and encourage more purchases at these times.

### 6  End-benefit effect

When an item purchased is a component part of a bigger decision, the price sensitivity will be influenced by the proportion of the item's cost relative to the whole ensemble. For example, a colleague, renowned for his search for value in most areas of his life, placed a deposit on a new Porsche Boxster at an agreed price. When the order came to be confirmed the salesman asked if he wanted leather seats. In the context of the whole package, the £2,000 cost seemed relatively small. An hour later the buyer commented, 'That's the fastest £2,000 I ever gave away!'

**Action:** Identify relatively low-cost items bought as part of a bigger transaction and ensure that margins and prices are uplifted by the halo potential of the package.

## 7  Shared-cost effect

The portion of the price paid by a buyer will influence his or her price sensitivity. Items may be subsidized by an employer or be tax deductible, or the cost may be shared in a joint venture.

**Action:** Identify whether some part cost of the product or service you are selling is borne by someone other than the customer. If so, price may be less important in the negotiation. Encourage joint purchasing, shared use and shared ownership among customers.

## 8  Fairness effect

Willingness to pay is strongly affected by an emotional perception of fairness. This is a strongly subjective area. Perceived fairness is linked to assumptions about the seller's profit margin and his or her motives. A feeling that a very large company is increasing prices to vulnerable individuals will be seen as unfair. This issue is explored in the Harvard Business School case study 'Coca-Cola's new vending machine'. An outcry met Coca-Cola's concept of raising the price on a hot day of cans of Coke sold through temperature-sensitive vending machines. The motives were interpreted as greed and exploitation. Consumers would be thirstier on a hot day, the rise in temperature occurred through no effort on the part of the company, children may have been sent by their parents with the exact coins normally required, and the Coke brand promise implies ubiquity and affordability. It was seen as unfair and the concept was abandoned. Yet an economic analysis would show that the refreshment value of a cold drink is greater on a hot day and by raising prices to reduce casual demand, availability from the vending machine for those strongly wishing to buy would be improved.

**Action:** Create communication strategies that attend to the perceived fairness of prices. For example, price increases may be justified by linking them to commitments to invest in future service improvements. Community activities also support positive image of companies and their other behaviours are perceived as 'fair'.

## 9  Framing effect

Nagle and Holden's book explains that framing is linked to prospect theory. People frame purchases as a bundle of gains and losses. Apparently customers place more weight on losses than on equal-sized gains. They are more price-sensitive when they perceive a price as a 'loss' to them rather than a foregone gain. For example, a lone traveller is considering two holiday packages for the same flight, destination and hotel:

**Holiday I**    £250 with a 10 percent single-person surcharge.
**Holiday II**   £300 with £25 discount for early booking.

The invoiced amount is £275 for both holidays but the surcharge is framed as a 'loss' where the discount is interpreted as a 'gain'.

**Action:** When prices vary between different occasions and different consumers, always express prices as discounts off the higher price charged. Avoid surcharges (see Chapter 11 for an exception to this rule). Always endeavour to surprise customers positively about price, rather than allowing unanticipated extras to create a negative effect. Finally, unbundle 'gains' by showing waived charges, discounts and free items separately. Bundle up 'losses' by presenting the total offering that the customer needs as a package.

There are other opportunities to influence willingness to pay. For example, buyers who cannot store a product are less price-sensitive and products that cannot be stored – like phone calls – will be less subject to price scrutiny than inventory items. What is seen is costed out. This may be a pricing opportunity for 'just-in-time' suppliers.

# Different customers, different sensitivity

Price sensitivity will vary between customers. Different segments exhibit differing awareness and consciousness of price. The author met Jonas Gunnarsson, Director of Market Research for the major Nordic supermarket group ICA, who described how he investigated consumer price perceptions of price levels in grocery stores. Interestingly, he used a 70-item 'shopping basket' to calibrate the actual ranking among ten grocery stores serving a particular Swedish community. He then surveyed consumers in this community for their perceptions. To quote his paper, 'The respondents who provided answers on average come very close to the actual store price index.' This is impressive. However, about one third of respondents ticked the 'don't know' box and another 12 percent omitted to answer the question on price levels. Thus a large number of shoppers felt for some reason that they were unable to make the comparison. We appear to have a group of consumers who are acutely aware of price levels and another group who have much lower price knowledge.

There are ways to take advantage of the highly price-sensitive segment of customers. Through their price sensitivity they can make your business more efficient:

▓ Clearing over-stocks – price-sensitive buyers respond quickly and surely to lower prices, so use them to clear unwanted surpluses.

▓ Managing supply variation – supply to price-sensitive buyers can be switched off when availability is constrained. Part of the price proposition is that supply cannot be guaranteed at low price levels.

Some customers will be highly aware of price and others will be much less sensitive. They will value products differently. How should we capture this value?

If every customer valued a product identically, it would make sense to sell at a single price. But they do not value products identically and therefore a single price brings two negative concepts.

Concept 1. Some customers valued your product more highly than your single price. They would have paid more and you left money on the table.

Concept 2. Some customers cannot or will not afford your single price. They would, however, have bought at a lower price that still delivered a return above your cost price. You lost profitable sales.

In Figure 4.2 a price of £50 is shown. Half the customers were willing to pay more and their value is not captured by the single price. However, half the customers would only purchase at a lower price and their sales potential has been lost at £50. Potential profit and potential sales have been lost through a single-price policy.

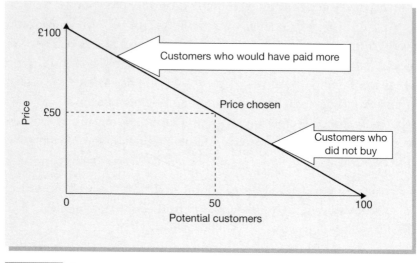

**Figure 4.2** Potential customers

A single-price policy has pitfalls. Writing in the *Financial Times*, Vanessa Holder (1996) points out that the high cost of accessing and processing price and cost information has led to some companies offering average prices for all customers. Examples are frequently found in utilities businesses. It stemmed from a belief in universal coverage. Postal companies chose an average price that tended to overcharge urban users whose density makes them lower cost to serve and subsidized the rural customers. Today, in competitive mail markets, the single-price policy risks attack from smart competitors who pick off the profitable urban addresses. Historically, credit card companies have overcharged low-risk customers and therefore new entrants can segment their approach and skim off the most attractive customers.

# The answer is price discrimination

Where different customers or groups of customers value products differently, the route to capturing this value is through differential pricing. Price discrimination means finding credible and sustainable ways to serve different segments at different prices. The economist, Arthur Pigou (1920) identified three levels of price discrimination:

- First degree – auction, haggling, bespoke prices
- Second degree – price/quantity, price/time relationship
- Third degree – segment or channel-based

## First-degree discrimination

First-degree price discrimination occurs when there is a unique price for every customer. The auction has been mentioned previously. Haggling in a bazaar is designed to identify the highest price each buyer will bear. Many business-to-business services will be based on bespoke prices per customer, driven by an assessment of economic value and a negotiated agreement.

A form of first-degree discrimination occurs in the market for used cars. As illustrated in Chapter 3, the car salesman conversing informally with a potential car buyer is assessing the customer's price sensitivity and the likely price that they might be able or willing to pay. Questions about work and their home are trying to establish available income. Questions about family and holidays are probing spend patterns. Questions about other cars they have looked at illicit knowledge of competition and market prices. Questions about address determine the convenience of the car dealer and hence the value to the buyer. All the questions result in a judgement on the deal price the salesman is prepared to offer. Different answers from different customers will receive varying amounts of money off the sticker price.

**Action:** Seek opportunities to create an individual price per customer. Train salespeople to assess accurately the specific value of the solution to the customer at that time. Software models can be developed to support this calculation and even demonstrate it to customers. Willingness to pay can be determined through a negotiation process. Train salespeople in effective negotiation to capture value created for customers.

## Second-degree discrimination

Second-degree occurs when there is a visible and obvious relationship between the volume purchased and the price. Bulk buying is a normal form of second-degree discrimination. Direct Golf UK supply golf equipment customized with brand logos to companies running corporate entertainment golf days. They have a discount scale (June 2005) for branded deluxe tins of golf tees:

| Number of tins | 50 | 100 | 250 | 500 | 1,000 |
|---|---|---|---|---|---|
| Price per tin | £7.49 | £7.29 | £6.99 | £6.49 | £5.99 |

Group discounts are a variant of bulk discount. The publisher, Penguin, offers a reading group 20 percent discount to buy five copies or more of the same book. The Manchester-based Hallé Symphony Orchestra gives group discounts with 10 percent off tickets for parties of ten, 15 percent for parties of 30 and 25 percent for groups larger than 50 persons.

Another form of second-degree discrimination is where a discount or surcharge is linked to the time of placing the order. Early buying discounts apply to cruises where customers paying six months or more in advance can earn up to 45 percent off the cabin price. Conversely, London theatres sell 'standby tickets' on the day of the performance at substantial discounts. It applies to the time of day where bars run 'Happy Hours', early in the evening with specially priced drinks to attract customers at quiet times. Retailers have end of season stock clearance.

### You've got to be 'fair'

It is necessary that customers see the condition for the discriminatory price as acceptable and fair. In the Coca-Cola vending machine example, price variation as a result of external temperature was not seen as an acceptable form of second-degree discrimination.

**Action:** Study the scales of volume discounts for opportunities to capture greater value. Look creatively at time-based pricing to capture more value from less flexible peak users and charge lower prices to encourage consumption at quieter times.

## Third-degree discrimination

Third-degree discrimination occurs when a segmented market permits watertight sales to one group at one price and to another group at another level with no arbitrage or transfer taking place between the segments.

Another form of third-degree discrimination occurs when different prices are charged through different sales channels.

For third-degree discrimination to succeed it must be acceptable to legal jurisdictions and either be invisible to customers or if visible, to appear justifiable. Customers appear to accept that on-line prices for air fares will be lower than fully serviced travel agent prices. They identify with different value obtained through the different channels.

The simplest form of price segmentation is effort-based. Cost conscious consumers will take time to read, understand and clip coupons from advertisements, carrying them in their wallets until the moment they are able to exchange them at point of purchase. The Beefeater restaurant chain mails out discount coupons invalid at busy holiday and weekend periods. These stimulate the cost conscious to make the effort to buy a weekday meal at a lower price. Other readers will simply be reminded of the restaurant and make a visit without the coupon, thus paying the regular price. Imposing effort for discounts screens out the lazy, busy and price insensitive.

## Demographic segments: persons of size pay more

Demographic segmentation is another accepted form of third-degree discrimination. Examples in consumer markets include: children under five free, student discount, senior citizen tickets, special offers for the non-waged. Hairdressers have a gender-based discrimination where women pay more than men to have their hair cut, and children pay even lower prices except on busy Saturday mornings. A relatively new form of price premium to a particular group is new rules for 'people of size' levied by Texas-based no-frills flier Southwest Airlines. Customers who are too fat to lower the seat armrest are required to pay for a second seat. The rules state clearly that two obese people travelling together may not share an extra seat – each must pay their own surcharge. A detailed advice section on the Southwest website warns customers that airports tend to be public places and advises large customers to avoid embarrassment by buying two seats just in case – the second seat will be refunded if they are able to lower the armrest on the plane!

Demographic segmentation also exists in business contexts. Conference organizers will offer lower prices to companies employing fewer than ten people. Banks have different charging scales for small/medium enterprises (SMEs) compared with international companies. Universities offer bursaries to participants from developing countries, business schools offer special rates on training programmes to employees of registered charities. In each instance there is an assessment of willingness to pay at different price levels and an identification of potential customers who could and will pay more to capture value from them. Price-sensitive or cost-constrained customers can be persuaded to buy with lower price levels restricted to their segment.

Other demographic segmentation may affect both consumer and business markets. For example, city prices may be higher when customers perceive rents and other costs to be greater. Alternatively, if vendors perceive aggressive urban competition, then city prices can be lower.

### Don't upset your best customers!

Companies may segment customers into existing and potential users. It is tempting to offer lower prices to potential buyers to encourage them to sample and become regulars. There are two disadvantages of discounts to new users. First, it may set a reference price for value in their minds that is too low to achieve ongoing sales. The lower prices may also become known to existing high-volume buyers – are they are being over-charged to subsidize customers buying low volumes? Promotional discounts to new mortgage borrowers have generated hostility from existing customers. Smarter companies offer *benefits* that apply only to new users. Free delivery, free installation, training will be irrelevant to an existing user.

### Different channel, different price

Customers accept that prices will vary by outlet type. A survey in *Marketing Magazine*, 22 September 2004, shows that typical price differences for identical items between supermarkets and convenience stores are around 4 percent. See Table 4.2.

**Table 4.2**    Supermarket and convenience store prices

|  | Supermarket | Convenience store | % premium |
|---|---|---|---|
| Coca-Cola 500ml | 79p (Sainsbury) | 85p (Sainsbury Local) | 7.6% |
| Heinz Baked Beans | 38p (Sainsbury) | 38p (Sainsbury Local) | nil |
| Hovis loaf | 72p (Tesco) | 75p (Tesco Express) | 4% |
| Kelloggs Corn Flakes | £1.24 (Tesco) | £1.29 (Tesco Express) | 4% |
| Lenor fabric conditioner 1 litre | 88p (Tesco) | 92p (Tesco Express) | 4.5% |

Source: *Marketing Magazine*, 22 September 2004.

Making unfounded assumptions about customer attitudes to price can easily lead to pricing errors. Frequently the Internet has acted as a force to drive down the prices that firms may charge. Yet, unusually, some firms are charging more on the web than in retail stores. For example, on-line transactions offer a benefit of anonymity that some customers value enough to pay a premium price. According to Rao, Bergen and Davis (2000) a study of 46 e-tailers of prescription drugs showed that Viagra (a medication for erectile dysfunction) and Propecia (treatment for male pattern baldness) were priced around 10 percent higher than drugstores.

Business-to-business customers are also motivated to avoid embarrassment where, for instance, currency movements can cause concerns. StoraEnso, the Swedish–Finnish paper business will price certain export contracts in the customer's currency. By assuming the currency risk, StoraEnso creates a value of certainty from exchange fluctuations for these customers. The message is that lower-priced channels may not be lower priced for every item if value is offered to certain segments of customers.

# Different segments, different brands

Where customers in different segments cannot be separated into 'watertight compartments', lower prices offered to one segment would be obvious to customers in segments who derive greater value from the product. This reference price effect limits the ability to capture this potential value. In these circumstances, separate products with separate brands are necessary. These may be lower-priced 'fighting brands' which appeal to the price-sensitive segments.

Tesco have three own-brand ranges. The 'Tesco' standard version is a mid-market offering. The 'Tesco finest' is a premium-priced luxury proposition with sales of £600 million in its own right. 'Tesco Value', launched in 1993, is a price-fighting offer. How does Tesco prevent leakage between the segments, and in particular prevent buyers of standard and premium ranges from trading down? Clive Humby and Terry Hunt (2003) give an insight in the book *Scoring Points*. Tesco has carefully designed the recipe and taste of their Value Margarine so that it will meet the basic needs of price-constrained shoppers who would otherwise buy elsewhere. The taste is not sufficiently palatable for more sophisticated tastes. By offering different products, Tesco capture the custom of the low-price payers and also capture the value from the high-price payers.

Capturing the value that you have created begins by understanding the price sensitivity of different buyers. With this knowledge, you can construct a price system or a segmented offer that allows more price-sensitive buyers to earn lower prices through a set of conditions that will exclude customers willing to pay a higher price. This process delivers higher overall returns. Start by gathering and interpreting information on customer price sensitivity.

## Chapter summary

- To achieve higher prices, you need to understand customer's price sensitivity. Generally when prices rise, fewer people will buy and they will buy less frequently – known as the price elasticity of demand.

- Price sensitivity varies between product categories and brands. It also varies over time. Nagle and Holden have identified nine effects to reduce price sensitivity. Actions are recommended.

- Price sensitivity also varies between customers. An average price will be less than some customers are willing to pay, so value is lost. The average price will also be too expensive for other customers and sales will be lost.

- The answer is price discrimination where prices differ between customers (first degree), or between purchase conditions (second degree) or between segments of customers and channels (third degree).

## Management questions for your business

- What is the pricing indifference band for each of our products and where have we scope to increase price within this band without losing sales?

- Are we sensitizing customers to prices in the market by drawing greater attention to price than to other elements of the marketing mix?

- How can we use a sense of novelty to reduce price sensitivity?

- Which of the nine effects to reduce price sensitivity could we deploy?

- How could we leverage positive benefits from our most price-sensitive customers?

## Going further – references and additional reading

Bijmolt, T. H. A., van Heerde, H. J. and Pieters, R. G. M. (2005) 'New empirical generalizations on the determinants of price elasticity', *Journal of Marketing Research*, May.

Chao, A. and Schor, J. B. (1998) 'Empirical tests of status consumption: evidence from women's cosmetics', *Journal of Economic Psychology*, 19(1).

Cohen, M. (1999) 'Pricing peculiarities of the UK petrol market', *Journal of Product and Brand Management*, 8.

Cram, A. (2001) *Customers that Count*, FT Prentice Hall, London – see especially Chapter 16 'Building barriers to exit'.

Gunnarsson, J. and Magi, A. (2001) 'How do consumers perceive the overall price-level of a grocery store – an exploratory field study', unpublished.

Holder, V. (1996) 'Knowing when the price is right', *Financial Times*, 29 April.

Humby, C. and Hunt, T. with Phillips, T. (2003) *Scoring Points – How Tesco is winning customer loyalty*, Kogan Page, London.

King, T. and Narayandas, D. (2000) 'Coca-Cola's new vending machine (A): Pricing to capture value or not?', Harvard Business School case study.

London, S. (2003) 'The real value in setting the right price', *Financial Times*, 11 September.

Marn, M., Roegner, G. V. and Zawada, C. C. (2004) 'Taking account of price sensitivity', in *The Price Advantage*, Wiley, Hoboken, NJ – see Chapter 4.

Monroe, K. B. (2003) *Pricing: Making Profitable Decisions*, McGraw Hill/Irwin, Burr Ridge, IL – see Part Two 'Prices and Demand'.

Nagle, T. and Holden, K. R. (2002) *The Strategy and Tactics of Pricing*, Prentice Hall, Upper Saddle River, NJ – see Appendix 4A 'Economics of price sensitivity'.

Pigou, A. (1920) *Economics of Welfare*, Macmillan & Co., London.

Rao, A. R., Bergen, M. E. and Davis, S. (2000) 'How to fight a price war', *Harvard Business Review*, March/April.

Sanchanta, M. (2005) 'Sieyu admits to mistakes in pricing policy', *Financial Times*, 31 January.

www.southwest.com/travel_center/cos_guidelines.html

# 5

# Customers behaving badly – how pricing can help

**case study 5.1**

How pricing leads to extraordinary customer behaviour – the IKEA experience

**The opening** of IKEA's new store in Edmonton, North London on 10 February 2005 was heralded by a promise of 24 hours of cut-price deals, including £325 leather sofas for £49 and double-bed frames for £30. IKEA expected 2,000 customers as the store opened its doors at midnight. Instead, over 6,000 bargain-hunters struggled to get in. With the car park full, desperate shoppers abandoned their vehicles on the main North Circular highway. Customers who had queued for 12 hours were angry when latecomers barged past them. Fights broke out. Customers quarrelled over possession of cut-price furniture. A man threatened a woman with a mallet. Nine ambulances battled through the abandoned cars. Six people were hospitalized and 20 were treated for heat exhaustion. Managers closed the shop after 30 minutes. Similar shopper riots have occurred in Moscow and Saudi Arabia. Pricing strategies can lead to extraordinary customer behaviour.

Pricing appears at first to be a rational discipline, where dispassionate buyers coolly evaluate prices. This can occur. Yet often prices spark irrational and emotional behaviour. To understand the ways that pricing can drive customer behaviour we will look at both negative and positive instances.

# Pricing that brings unsatisfactory behaviour

The pricing strategy adopted by a company can effectively train its customers to behave in negative and unprofitable ways. For example, Thomas T. Nagle and George E. Cressman (2002) criticize business-to-business companies operating reactive pricing processes. Without formal pricing structures and strict criteria for discounts, they allow price negotiation as long as deals meet some minimum profit level. The intention is to be flexible and responsive to changing market dynamics. The result can be expensive. Regular customers soon learn that aggressive negotiating achieves larger and more frequent discounts. Smart buyers institute policies that drive deeper discounts – requiring salespeople to deal with procurement departments, limiting supplier contact with satisfied users. They allocate wedges of business to competitors to increase leverage. They form buying co-operatives. The company has taught its customers the benefits of price resistance – rewarding them with discounts if they will not agree immediately. 'Good customers' have been incentivized to become 'bad customers'.

The answer here is to re-establish prices and price structures that are respected by customers, who see identifiable value and perceive integrity that creates trust. It is a difficult transition and it is therefore better to avoid the situation in the first place.

In consumer markets, price promotions can also encourage unsatisfactory behaviour. The researchers, Srinivasan, Pauwels, Hanssens and Dekimpe (2002) studied seven years of scanner data covering 25 product categories and 75 brands from Dominick's Finer Foods, the Number Two grocery retailer in the Chicago area. They discovered that a typical one-week retail price promotion creates an immediate increase in revenue for the manufacturer, followed by a balancing negative impact over the following few weeks as customers migrate to normal brands and rival brands retaliate with counter promotions. They discovered that the persistent effect was zero as sales returned to the baseline after the sixth week. For the retailer, the immediate effect was a revenue loss while the long-term pattern reverts to the baseline also after the sixth week. However, they warn of the risk that buyers may refuse to purchase heavily promoted items once they return to the higher price. In the customer's perception, a reference price has been set that has a substantive effect. The impact on customer behaviour is that it becomes hard for customers of, say, a television to buy at regular price once they have noticed the promotional price.

## Pricing to help customers behave profitably

Of course, pricing can be used to encourage customers to behave profitably.

Historically, water supply to domestic households in the UK was always charged at a flat rate based indirectly on property values. With no correlation between the amount charged and usage, customers had no incentive to conserve water. Thus, in periods of drought, action had to be taken to impose on all customers bans on the use of hose-pipes. In the 1980s, pricing began to be used as a mechanism to encourage responsible behaviour. Water companies began requiring water meters in all new homes. Existing households were encouraged to install water meters, and a long-term programme began to bring about the linking of usage and payment, to encourage profitable behaviour.

Rules to achieve profitable behaviour
Number 1. Link usage to price – avoid average pricing.

## Charge them for what they *don't* eat!

The Oriental City Food Court, 399 Edgware Road, in North London offers an open Chinese buffet with self-service for a fixed meal price of £15 per head. The factor most impacting on profit, once the price has been set, is the degree of wasted food. Therefore, to encourage good behaviour, the restaurant has a second dimension to its pricing scale: wastage above a token amount on any plate is charged at £5 per 200gm. With a penalty for wasting food, diners tend to take small portions and refill with dishes they enjoy. Good behaviour is supported by the pricing structure.

There is a cost to a dentist when a patient misses an appointment. This 'bad behaviour' on the part of the patient results in extra administrative time for rebooking. Treatments for other patients will be needlessly delayed. To encourage 'good behaviour', a dentist in Monmouth who charges £70 for a first appointment, penalizes missed appointments with a charge of £85.

Rules to achieve profitable behaviour
Number 2. Penalize waste – add a surcharge.

## The ultimate price promise

Falling prices of successive generations of electronic equipment has given a perverse incentive to prospective customers to hold back until the price comes down. The Carphone Warehouse – one of the UK's leading retailers of mobile phones – has identified this barrier to purchase, overcoming it with a creative approach: the ultimate price promise.

If you buy a mobile phone from the Carphone Warehouse, 90 days later, the company's computer compares the price paid and the current price. If the price has fallen, a voucher for the difference will automatically be mailed to the buyer. This voucher can be redeemed in store for a phone accessory or put towards a larger transaction. In the book *Uncommon Practice* (Milligan and Smith, 2002), the Chief Executive Officer, Charles Dunstone comments, 'In the last 14 months we've given away £10 million to customers, but they are astounded when they get it; they can't believe that any company would do that.' For the customer, the barrier to purchase has been lifted. There is every reason to go ahead and buy today. The Carphone Warehouse has found a pricing tool to encourage profitable behaviour.

Rules to achieve profitable behaviour
Number 3. Break barriers to purchase: remove the threat
of falling prices

## Mini-bar barrier lifted

Three- and four-star hotel rooms are routinely equipped with mini-bars containing a selection of beers, wines and spirits. Research has indicated that customers undervalue the convenience of having a drink an arm's length away. Mini-bars are seen as expensive and this discourages guests from patronizing them. The Art Hotel, Kielbasnicza 20, Wroclaw in Poland has a strategy to alter perceptions. In this hotel, the room rate includes the price of the *first* drink from the mini-bar. Guests discover the convenience value by savouring this first drink and the barrier to taking subsequent paid-for drinks is broken.

Rules to achieve profitable behaviour
___
Number 4. Break barriers to purchase by bundling in
a sample.

## Pricing that impacts consumption

Pricing strategies can also influence patterns of consumption positively. Consumption is vital because people are unlikely to buy more until they have consumed the initial purchase. The impact may be greater than this. Consider a football club with a season ticket offer. If season ticket holders do not attend matches, then potential revenue is lost for sales of programmes, burgers, hot dogs, soft drinks, clothing and other souvenirs. How can pricing encourage consumption? Imagine two people who pay the same fee to join a health club. In a 2002 study, John Gourville and Dilip Soman of Harvard Business School found that someone who pays $50 per month is more likely to attend regularly (and renew their membership the following year) than the person making a single payment of $600. The single payment member will feel a need to get value for money and use the club heavily initially. As the pain of the $600 payment fades, his drive to get value will lessen. By contrast, the member paying monthly has a regular reminder on their bank statement to continue working out, and regular users renew. Renewal and repeat custom is profitable. Making customers aware of their spend will encourage them to get value, leading to repeat purchase patterns. So pricing is able to impact on consumption behaviours profitably.

Rules to achieve profitable behaviour
___
Number 5. Regular payments encourage more consumption
(and repurchase) than heavy up-front costs.

# Ten dollar bills feel more than $100 on the card

The research by Gourville and Soman (2002) also flagged up the link between payment methods and perceptions of cost. They discovered that consumption is driven more by *perceptions of cost* than actual paid-for cost. A cash transaction involves counting out the notes, handing them over, receiving and counting the change. The more stages in the transaction the greater the impression of magnitude. A credit card payment involves just a quick tap of a PIN. So a purchase with cash will feel more expensive than a purchase on the card. Moreover, buyers will remember the precise cost of a cash transaction far more often than they can remember the exact amount on the credit card slip. Thus the impression of commitment with a cash purchase will increase the determination to consume the paid-for product. In a study of theatre no-shows, the ratio of credit card payers failing to turn up was ten times greater than the committed cash buyers.

Rules to achieve profitable behaviour

Number 6. Encouraging cash payment increases consumption. Encouraging credit card decreases awareness of price, perceptions of cost and determination to consume.

# Early payment, less commitment

Timing of payment is another factor that impacts on awareness of the amount paid and hence determination to consume the product or service. Payment at or near the time of consumption increases attention to the product's cost, raising the likelihood that the product will be consumed and not wasted. Gourville and Soman (2002) say that season ticket holders will be less diligent in attending events than buyers paying shortly before the event. The further ahead in time you pay for an event ticket, statistically, the greater the probability of failure to attend. This knowledge can be used in yield management, by forecasting attendance, assessing support staff numbers and, perhaps, by overselling to balance the no-show element.

---
Rules to achieve profitable behaviour
---
Number 7. Encouraging late payment increases
consumption. Encouraging early payment decreases
perceptions of cost, awareness of price and
determination to consume.

The conclusion drawn by Gourville and Soman (2002) is that early payment schemes, credit plans and activities to draw attention away from price may increase demand by making customers less conscious of the cost. However, an awareness of cost can have a positive impact on determination to consume, which is correlated with repeat buying. Either way, pricing can impact behaviour significantly.

The rules to achieve profitable behaviour are:

1  Link usage to price – avoid average pricing.

2  Penalize waste – add a surcharge.

3  Break barriers to purchase: remove the threat of falling prices.

4  Break barriers to purchase by bundling in a sample.

5  Use regular payments to encourage more consumption (and repurchase) than heavy up-front costs.

6  Use cash payment to increase consumption, credit cards to decrease perceptions of cost (and determination to consume).

7  Use late payment to increase consumption, early payment to decrease perception of costs (and determination to consume).

# Men don't read price tags

At the retail level, there are gender differences in price behaviours. Paco Underhill (2000) in his book *Why We Buy*, noted that men are markedly more reluctant to inspect price tickets or ask for prices than female shoppers. For low-cost items, they may buy irrespective of price. For high-ticket products aimed at masculine buyers, where price is an important factor in the purchase decision, bold price labelling is necessary. This can be seen, for example, in consumer electronic products. If they cannot readily see the price, they may well walk away.

Older people, whose eyesight is less effective than younger people, may be unable to read small print price tags. Likewise, seeing low-contrast black print on red labels is difficult as the cornea yellows with age. Being reluctant to draw attention to their deteriorating sight, senior citizens tend to move on, rather than ask. For both groups, clear labelling will have sales benefits.

Consumers may not always be analytical in their pricing behaviour. Some companies have tried to exploit this. For example, there is an expectation that big packs are relatively less expensive, in that they will cost less per gram. Yet sometimes retailers charge higher relative prices for jumbo sizes. In a *Wall Street Journal* article of August 2002, McCarthy describes how Wal-Mart shoppers could save 30 cents and gain seven ounces by purchasing four small cans of Van Camps pork and beans rather than a single large one. Strategies that exploit the consumer's mathematical shortcomings may bring temporary benefits. However, the long-term risk is that the perception of price integrity will be damaged leading to reluctance to trust pricing information across the range.

Trust is vital in achieving positive behaviours. With trust, people become less conscious of prices and more willing to pay the amount sought.

## Price stimulates behaviours – manage that knowledge well

The evidence is clear that price can stimulate particular positive or negative behaviours. It is wise for firms to determine how best to bring about positive reactions. In doing this they should ensure that they are not exploiting customer vulnerabilities in the short term so that the long-term effect is a breach of trust in the price structure.

## Chapter takeaways

- Contrary to expectation, pricing can stimulate behaviours that may not be rational. Some of these may have a negative profit affect. For example, price promotions may set reference price levels that discourage future purchases at full price.

■ There are seven ways that pricing can encourage profitable behaviours. These draw on social psychology.

■ Customer psychology could be used to exploit customer vulnerabilities. The better long-term strategy is to operate with price integrity so that trust is retained.

## Management questions for your business

■ Are we incentivizing good customers to behave badly over price?

■ Do price promotions provide customers with reference points that work to our disadvantage?

■ Can we use the seven rules to make customers behave profitably?

■ Does our pricing increase short-term demand, only to depress long-term consumption?

■ Are we pricing with integrity?

## Going further – references and additional reading

Cram, T. and Stilliard, B. (1996) 'Securing relationships', *Financial Times*, 23 August.

Dickinson, H. (2005) 'Chaos in IKEA may be a taste of things to come', *Marketing Magazine*, 2 March.

Gourville, J. and Soman, D. (2002) 'Pricing and the psychology of consumption', *Harvard Business Review*, September.

McCarthy, M. J. (2002) 'Taking the value out of value-sized', *Wall Street Journal*, 14 August.

Milligan, A. and Smith, S. (eds) (2002) *Uncommon Practice: People who deliver a great brand experience*, FT Prentice Hall, London.

Nagle, T. T. and Cressman, G. E. (2002) 'Don't just set prices, manage them', *Marketing Management*, November/December.

Srinivasan, S., Pauwels, K., Hanssens, D. M. and Dekimpe, M. (2002) 'Who benefits from price promotions?', *Harvard Business Review*, September.

Underhill, P. (2000) *Why We Buy*, Texere, New York, NY.

# 2

# Competitors: smarter ways to outwit them

# 6

# Standing out from the crowd – pricing's role in positioning and differentiation

---

**case study 6.1**

## Using price to reposition a brand – ICA's message to Sweden

**The ICA Group** is one of the Nordic region's largest retail companies employing over 40,000 people across stores in Sweden, Norway, Denmark, Estonia, Lithuania and Latvia. With over 1,600 stores in Sweden, ICA holds a significant position in its heartland.

As the mainstream brand leader, it is important to convey to customers that they are receiving good value. New, low-priced grocery competitors, like Netto, have entered the market. The availability of lower prices (albeit on a narrower range), effectively re-positioned ICA in the minds of customers as being more expensive. To address this, ICA launched its 'Price offensive' in March 2005. A press release from the Head office at Solna, near Stockholm, announced, 'ICA stores across Sweden are gearing up to slash prices on 2,400 staple items'. A TV campaign announced that prices had been dropped permanently. Jonas Gunnarsson, Director, Marketing Research, showed me dramatic pink posters highlighting lower prices on regularly purchased items like ham, margarine, pizza and light bulbs.

The aim is to reposition the price perception of the ICA brand and to make it clear to customers that prices in their local store have come down. They intend to maintain the existing positive perceptions of

▶

product quality. The brand value they want to affect is the feeling that you can make a good bargain at ICA. To succeed as a mainstream brand, price is a key component in the company's positioning.

*Source: ICA Annual Report* (www.ica.se) meeting with Jonas Gunnarsson.

# Up-market or down-market?

When companies are monopoly suppliers, they have no competition and need only assess the value to potential customers. Do they have the ability to pay? What is their willingness to buy? How will price influence the level of their demand? Companies are rarely alone in their market with their customers, they must consider competitors (see Figure 6.1).

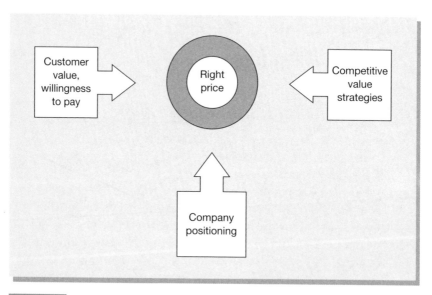

**Figure 6.1**  **Three pointers to the right price**

Competitor offerings allow customers to make comparisons. Customers will position brands relative to each other. Is a brand 'up-market' or 'down-market'? The position that a brand occupies in customers' minds will therefore partly be defined by competitors. A credible premium position is associated in the mind of a customer with a higher price. For example, Miele advertise their washing machines with the slogan 'Anything else is a compromise' and hence their price is higher than mainstream Hotpoint-branded washing machines.

## What is positioning?

Positioning is what the company stands for in the eyes of customers relative to competitors (as shown in Figure 6.2).

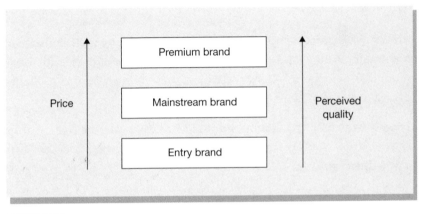

**Figure 6.2**    Positioning is what the brand stands for relative to competitors

In the global car rental market, Hertz position themselves as Number 1. Avis position themselves as the Number 2 who must try harder. Thus Hertz would be expected to occupy the premium price position in the market justified by multi-locations, large fleets and up-to-the-minute models. Avis prices must be close to Hertz (no higher, just a little below) and above the lower-rank players to be seen as a keen contender with Hertz (as shown in Table 6.1). Other companies are likely to pitch their prices below international leaders.

Price plays a key role in positioning. It is a clear, ascertainable aspect and it instantly places a brand on the field.

| Table 6.1 | Price positioning: quoted prices for a three-day rental for a medium family car, Manchester airport June 2005 | | |
|---|---|---|---|
| Hertz | Avis | AutoEurope | Alamo |
| £132.50 | £112.50 | £95.99 | £87.00 |
| Index: 100 | Index 85 | Index 72 | Index 66 |

Source: travelsupermarket.com.

# Price – a quality indicator . . . and more

## How price can communicate the position on the quality spectrum?

Armed with a price comparison, a customer can draw conclusions about the nature of the brand choice. Which is the 'cheap and cheerful' basic product? Who offers the standard version? Which is the premium player?

The UK wine retailer, Oddbins, implies a link between price and quality: the search facility for standard wines on its website www.oddbins.co.uk offers three options:

■ less than £5.00

■ £5–£10.00

■ over £10.00

There is a theory among tailors that the pricing of bespoke men's suits coincides with the pricing of bottles of wine, only with two noughts added at the end. An £8.00 bottle of Chablis could be compared with a luxurious lightweight, £800.00 designer suit. Just as you would doubt the quality of a sub-£3.00 bottle of wine, so a suit costing less than £300.00 poses potential sartorial risks. Richard Rawlinson (1997), writing in the *Financial Times*, drew the conclusion that the message of this pricing yardstick is that you get what you pay for.

The price–quality relationship is the basis of this yardstick. In markets where quality is hard to judge from other external indicators, price assumes a significant importance in positioning. New entrants in business-to-business markets must determine where they will price themselves compared with existing suppliers – below if they have a simpler offering, above if they provide a superior product or service.

When they recruit, companies are in effect 'employment brands'. They use 'price', or the salary they are offering, as a form of positioning. To confirm their desired market status, some companies pay top quartile salaries to executives. The intention is to make themselves attractive in recruiting and retaining the best candidates and distinguish themselves from lesser companies.

Price can communicate a company's position on the quality spectrum. It can also do more than this.

## How price can convey accessibility

A lower than expected price is able to convey accessibility and afford-ability. The reputation of Swatch as a stylish international brand has been confirmed over time since its launch in 1983. The Swiss Corpo-ration for Microelectronics and Watchmaking Industries (SMH) created Swatch as a fashion response to aggressive price-based competition from Japanese quartz timepieces. So successful has been the Swatch, it has now given its name to the parent group which has grown to be the largest manufacturer and distributor of finished watches in the world. The Swatch brand itself has quality credentials – Swatch kept time at the 2004 Athens Olympic Games and will again be the official timekeeper for the Beijing Olympic Games in 2008. It is a fashion statement. Yet you can buy a Swatch for under €40.

The prices have deliberately been chosen to position Swatch as an affordable fashion accessory. The prices do not exclude buyers on small budgets. However, limited production runs and low prices mean that availability is limited. To buy the Swatch you like, you must buy it when you see it. Price is part of the brand positioning.

## How price can convey that it is easy to do business

There are some categories of purchasing where price bargaining is customary. An example is buying a car. In the USA, particularly, overproduction and over-pricing has led to constant discounting and deal-making behaviour from savvy customers. Some customers enjoy the cut and thrust of negotiation. Other customers dread this need to haggle and are reluctant to buy for fear of getting a poor deal. There is an opportunity to position a company as differentiated from other brands.

The Saturn brand positioning is 'people first'. The brand offers a fixed price no hassle, no haggle sales policy. The price conveys the idea that the company is easy to do business with.

## How price can reassure

Price can also be deployed to give a brand positioning of market awareness and customer fairness. Customers may fear that the product they are planning to buy could be on sale elsewhere at a lower price. Price guarantees can reassure customers that they cannot buy for less.

An early example of this commitment comes from the UK department store, John Lewis. Their slogan, 'Never knowingly undersold', was coined in the 1920s by John Spedan Lewis, the son of the founder. The word 'knowingly' communicates that they endeavour to identify and match competitor prices – the onus is on the retailer. Nevertheless, the guarantee means that if you can show that you could have bought the same thing cheaper elsewhere, they will refund the difference. Thus the John Lewis pricing message supports a positioning of trustworthiness through knowledge of the market and a commitment to 'fair' prices.

## How price conveys security

Security is another element of brand positioning that can be conveyed through pricing. Market entrants often have the advantages of novelty, nimbleness and flexibility. Thus, for incumbents, the alternative virtues of security of supply and security of buying terms can give a differentiation.

British Gas, the leading UK energy supplier, has positioned itself as safe, reliable and secure. The implication is that customers will not receive unpleasant surprises. In keeping with this positioning, during 2005 British Gas offered its domestic gas customers the opportunity to avoid gas price increases for two years. A 'price protection' premium of 3.5 percent removed the uncertainty of future price rises. British Gas reported in March 2005 that 65,000 customers per week were signing up for this security.

Similarly, business-to-business markets also feature long-duration contracts with fixed prices or agreed price change mechanisms which communicate security for the long term.

## How price can convey differentiation

Where prices are significantly different from standard, this can alert the customer to an element of differentiation.

Bananas are one of Europe's favourite fruits and sales have grown rapidly. At the same time, media stories have highlighted poor living conditions of banana growers. In response, the concept of Fairtrade bananas emerged. Producers would receive a 'fair price' for their produce. In 1996 these bananas were only available in Germany, Belgium and Switzerland through small independent outlets. Consumers responded positively and, by 2002, 20 percent of Switzerland's bananas bore the Fairtrade identifier. Fairtrade bananas were first sold in the UK in January 2000, initially by retailers J. Sainsbury and the Co-op. The fruits were imported from independent producers in Costa Rica rather than multi-national corporations such as Dole, Del Monte, Bonito and Chiquita. The Fairtrade Foundation set up the scheme to enable shoppers to buy bananas knowing that the producers had received a fair price and a fair deal. The Fairtrade logo confirms that the growers will have good working and living conditions and are not at risk from harmful pesticides.

Fairtrade bananas are now available in all the major UK supermarkets. Sales reached 18 million kilos in 2003 and 25 million kilos in 2004 – a growth of 43 percent. The price is around £1.12 to £1.24 compared with a typical price of 74p for standard bananas. The Fairtrade position is that the bananas are all the more enjoyable when you know that the extra 40 pence per kilo is going to the growers. The 60 percent price premium says that these bananas are different.

In the industrial market, Caterpillar Inc., the Illinois-based manufacturer of heavy equipment, uses price as a means to reinforce its differentiation. Without a price premium their claim to superiority would not be credible. On their website they boldly state, 'We plan to remain the leader and continue to help you meet your needs with our equipment, with the best distribution and product support system in any capital goods industry and the continual introduction and updating of products.' Their differentiation is 'maximum uptime' for operators of their heavy equipment. More uptime means more value for the operator, and Caterpillar's pricing captures some of that value for the company. It also acts as confirmation of the differentiation.

## How price conveys exclusivity

Exclusivity is an intangible quality sought by some up-market consumer brands. The intended positioning is that the product in question is rare, and should be prized. It is certainly not for everyone. Price can support such a position.

Maserati is a sporting Italian car marque, whose aficionados boast of the 1929 land speed record and close to 500 Grand Prix and other successes in a 30-year history of works teams. Today, equipped with Ferrari-built engines, the 400bhp Quattroporte, the Coupe GT and the Spyder have the rare ability to make pedestrians turn to watch them pass. Annual vehicle production is around 5,000 vehicles with capacity able to rise to only 10,000. This limited scale makes Maserati a truly exclusive brand, in competition with luxury brands, like BMW and Mercedes, who sell hundreds of thousands of vehicles. The price can communicate such exclusivity – in most European markets Maserati models are priced at 10–20 percent premium over the equivalent BMW.

The Janet Reger brand proves its exclusivity through an even greater premium for its lingerie. The founder, Janet Phillips, had a family background in clothing, her grandfather ran a textile factory and her parents made bras from Rayon off-cuts during the war. She studied 'Contour Fashion' at Leicester Polytechnic in the 1950s. After her marriage to Peter Reger in 1961, she began to design lingerie. In the mid-1960s the Janet Reger range was launched in London. The camisole tops, bras, pants, suspenders and negligees were all in pretty colours and luxurious fabrics, quite a contrast to the sensible nylon knickers and firm brassieres in white or cream previously worn by British women.

The brand exclusivity was confirmed with news of a Saudi princess spending £50,000 on lingerie in a couple of hours. Celebrities like Bianca Jagger bought Janet Reger underwear. The actress Joan Collins paraded the brand in the 1978 film *The Stud* and the legend was confirmed with a line in a Tom Stoppard play, 'Don't get your Janet Regers in a twist.'

Today, a long Katrina nightdress on the website www.janetreger.co.uk can cost £362 and luxury briefs are priced at more than £70. By comparison, briefs from La Senza, another up-market lingerie brand, range from £4.00 to £10.00. The exclusivity of the Janet Reger brand is supported by the price.

## How price conveys indulgence

High prices relative to competitors can be a component in communicating a message of indulgence. Obviously the product, service or experience will need to justify the price premium, and the premium percentage must be credible. However, at the point of purchase, the price acts as confirmatory evidence of intended superiority.

Hill Station manufactures super-premium ice-cream in Calne, Wiltshire, England. It supports its position with super-premium prices. The company was founded in 1994 by two former JP Morgan bankers and *Financial Times* reported its flotation on the Alternative Investment Market (AIM) in October 2004.

Super-premium ice-cream differs from standard ice-cream on a number of dimensions. Standard ice-cream is made from butter rather than cream giving it a fat content of 6–12 percent. Air added to the mixture to make it soft and light can be up to two-thirds of total volume. Brands are typically priced at £2 per litre. At the other end of the scale, super-premium brands, such as Häagen-Dazs and Ben & Jerry's, are made from milk or high-fat cream giving a fat content of 16–18 percent. Air content can be as little as one-fifth of total volume and it is unlikely to contain emulsifiers, stabilizers or other artificial ingredients. Typical prices are

£6 per litre, or £3 per 500ml container. Hill Station chose to convey a message with a recommended retail price of £3.95 per 500ml tub, around 30 percent above rivals. Its aim was to set high expectations for the quality of the brand – if it is more expensive than well-known super-premium brands, it must be a real indulgence.

The super-premium positioning is sustained by being stocked in outlets associated with indulgence, such as Harrods and Harvey Nichols, by being served in Virgin Upper Class, by featuring on menus in better London restaurants and by their pricing level.

## How price can convey aspiration

Premium pricing can give an up-market positioning to a new brand like Hill Station. For Lacoste, a luxury brand with a chequered history, things were tougher. As we saw in Chapter 1, sales in the USA in the 1990s were slipping, and licensee General Mills cut costs to maintain margins, using inferior fabrics and manufacturing techniques. Poorer quality reduced sales, putting further pressure on cost saving. The aspirational brand was no long anything to aspire to. When former Levi's executive, Robert Siegel, took over the loss-making Lacoste in 2001, he increased prices and introduced restyled men's shirts and shapelier women's shirts. In his view, a cheaper sales tag would not reflect the quality, nor allow continued product investment. The price rose, the quality rose and sales rose by 125 percent in 2004. In the luxury clothing market, higher prices contributed significantly to the aspirational positioning of the brand.

So, there are nine ways that market positioning is supported by price:

1 quality

2 accessibility

3 easy to do business

4 reassurance

5 security

6 differentiation

7 exclusivity

**8** indulgence

**9** aspiration.

# Dynamic market . . . relativities change

However, positioning through price presents a challenge. The position is illustrated not by the absolute price, but by the price *relative* to other choices. As these reference prices change, then the positioning itself can be changed. What was an acceptable premium price can become unacceptable when a competitor drops the price or improves the performance of a substitute brand.

In September 2004, two leading consumer multi-nationals, Unilever and Colgate-Palmolive issued profits warnings on the same day. Both needed to invest more marketing money in communicating the benefits of their brands in the face of strong competition. This competition came from branded rivals and also from supermarket own brands. Adam Jones (2004), writing in the *Financial Times* reported Unilever's comment that it had lost market share in ice-cream to own-label products from supermarkets and hard discounters. The company was also finding it difficult to persuade consumers to pay extra for its branded margarine.

JP Morgan analyst, Arnaud Langlois observed that branded consumer goods companies have not realized that, in this tough environment, the prices of many of their products are 'simply too high'. He added that 'for brands to become relevant again, their prices will have to go down'.

The alternative option (see Figure 6.3) is for the premium to be better justified by product characteristics, emotional associations and effective communication.

Look to Unilever's successful deodorant business. Brands like Axe (Lynx in the UK) offer functional product benefits, infer emotional qualities and communicate both effectively. When teenage girls are supremely sophisticated, the teenage boys who aspire to impress them need all the confidence that they can spray on. Axe is able to provide this confidence by understanding every aspect of the teenage experience. First, the

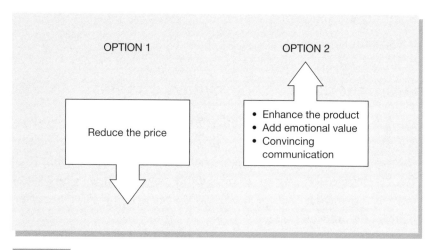

**Figure 6.3**    Premium position under attack

deodorant spray itself gives confidence by effectively preventing odour. Second, everything – the pack appearance, the sound made by the spray and the aroma – supports the message. Even the simple actuator that propels the deodorant has been designed to contribute to confidence building. The slide and press mechanism responds quickly and efficiently. Aesthetically, the button feels right. Finally the award-winning advertising convinces the target market that they can be confident with the brand. One television advert showed a spontaneous meeting in a supermarket that lead to romance – you never know when you will need that deodorant protection! Axe delivers on all dimensions and customers willingly pay the price. A premium positioning must be supported and sustained by the rest of the proposition.

## You've got to be different: ban commodity thinking

Credible positioning depends on differentiation and again this must be dynamic. In other words, the difference must be maintained even as competitors attack. Inferior competitors will try to draw parallels. Yet in the customer's mind there must be clear, continuing and relevant differentiation in order to justify higher prices.

If you think you have a 'price problem', it may be more to do with the rest of the proposition failing to justify the price in comparison with rivals.

Everything can be differentiated. As soon as the customer believes that two products offer the same benefits, then commodity buying comes into play and price becomes the decider. Ban commodity thinking. Focus on differences.

## Is water a commodity?

Water is not a commodity. Bottled water brands have always faced low-priced competition – namely tap water – yet have seen remarkable growth in the past decade by differentiation and a focus on benefits. According to Mark Sweney (2004), writing in *Marketing Magazine*, private label brands of bottled water from supermarkets grew by 19 percent in the UK market in 2003. Yet Danone Waters launched Volvic Revive, a mineral water-based sports drink, and sales grew by 29 percent in 2003.

Other major brands focused on different qualities. Evian's Nomad bottle, aimed at outdoor types, carries a belt clip, while Lakeland Willows' Salacin water contains naturally occurring aspirin to combat heart disease. If they offer genuine value to consumers, such benefits allow producers to sustain or raise prices.

## Is concrete a commodity?

Concrete is not a commodity. Agilia from Lafarge is differentiated concrete which is self-compacting and self-levelling. It achieves good consolidation without internal or external vibration. According to the Lafarge website, Agilia offers benefits to contractors, architects, engineers and owners. These include the cosmetic benefit of a smooth flat finish, financial advantages of speed and reduced labour costs, performance benefits of better noise insulation and safety factors as a result of full contact between reinforcing steel and concrete. Agilia commands a price premium.

## Is plastic a commodity?

Plastics are not commodities. In the business-to-business sector, Polymerland, part of GE Plastics, supplies resins to designers and manufacturers of plastic products. The properties of the resins must match precisely the required characteristics of the end product – a mobile phone, for example. It must also match the needs of the manufacturing process. According to Thomke and Hippel, Polymerland differentiates its plastics business by making available 30 years' in-house knowledge and expertise on a website. The site is password-protected and allows registered users access to company data sheets, engineering skills and even simulation software. This perceptive benefit of risk reduction through simulation and information supports the customer's choice to specify GE Plastics in a market which could be seen as a commodity.

# Differentiation is the lifeblood – there are three types

Differentiation from competitors creates the opportunity for companies to charge higher prices than rivals. If water, concrete and plastic can be differentiated, you can believe in scope for every product to be made different in some dimension.

Examples of dimensions of value include:

- specific product attributes which increase effectiveness in use
- dependability, continuity of supply
- certainty
- convenience and accessibility
- tailored information
- status
- emotional relevance
- personalization
- rewards.

Consider which of these could make a product or service somehow unique. Systematically seek ways to make your product or service different from the rest. There is a three-way structure for this method.

Michael Marn, Eric V. Roegner and Craig C. Zawada (2004), writing in *The Price Advantage* offer three categories of benefit that may deliver differentiation-based price advantage. These are:

■ functional

■ process

■ relationship.

## Get the basics right, that'll support higher prices

Functional benefits derive from product and service specification and are usually performance attributes. Examples would be power, speed, purity, absorption rate, longevity, durability, reliability, resale value, machine efficiency, labour-saving advantages. The task is to identify functional benefits that are capable of differentiating a product or service. These functional benefits must be meaningful to customers. Patent protection or superior design capability is needed to provide a continuing advantage. Nike stays ahead by working with leading athletes in the sports where it aims to excel.

Conventional wisdom suggests that major functional benefits are 'table stakes' in many mature businesses and that all the players operate at the acceptable level. These brands then differentiate using unique but minor functional benefits. Professors Barwise and Meehan (2004) recommend another way. Their research has shown much customer dissatisfaction with what might be described as the basics of a brand promise. In their view, customers are less interested in new elements of brand differentiation and would prefer to see companies delivering the fundamentals well.

Barwise and Meehan cite Toyota whose success is built on reliability, where other less profitable marques seek excitement and panache as differentiators. Cemex, the Mexican cement company, focuses on fast delivery for its Readimix concrete. On the other hand, UK banks offer ever-more esoteric loan packages, when most customers simply want a cheque processed in less than three days. Barwise and Meehan offer a first priority: simply to become demonstrably better than the competition at giving the customer what matters to them most.

## Make it easier, achieve higher prices

Process benefits are those that make the interchange between buyer and seller more convenient, easier, faster, reliable or simply more pleasant. Examples are superior product cataloguing, computer-based specification guides, automated reordering systems, simplified payment-processes, better-trained telephone agents. Again the requirement for pricing success is to find ways of delivering continuing superiority in the delivery of this benefit.

To command a long term price premium, a company must focus on ways of staying ahead on its chosen dimensions. For example, a cross-channel ferry focusing on easy-booking via its website should invest more time and money in upgrading its booking system, so that it is always faster, more intuitive and offers more legible graphics than its competitors.

## Build a relationship, earn higher prices

Relationship benefits are built around intangible and emotional aspects. How does the buyer feel as a result of his or her association with the seller? How do the brand values impact on the customer's self-perception? Other examples are loyalty rewards, status and recognition, privileged information or access to a user-group.

To earn higher prices, the relationship must bring emotional value to the buyer. It is easier to illustrate differences in relationships than it is to differentiate mature products. Thus, much thought is given to building long-term relationships with key customers. Sincerity and a consistent approach in both good and bad times bring credibility. In business-to-business, key account managers are appointed to co-ordinate relationships. In the hospitality industry, Marriott Hotels have developed Marriott Rewards to recognize guest loyalty, with specific advantages like upgrades and monthly billing that make them first choice for frequent executive travellers.

## Looking for new points of difference

Finally, for a company seeking new points of difference, MacMillan and McGrath (1997) suggest in the *Harvard Business Review* that the most effective approach is to scrutinize the customer's relationship with the product chronologically from the first to the last. At the outset, how does the customer originally become aware of the product? Can this be enhanced? How might word-of-mouth referral be encouraged, for example? How do new customers find the product and could this be made easier? The process continues through the actual usage of the product to the ultimate disposal of it. Paying close attention to the sequence of steps can frequently find a better way. And the better way commands a better price.

The following list – based on MacMillan and McGrath (1997) – summarizes how you can derive fresh insights by examining and interrogating the consumption chain:

▪ How do people become aware of the need?

▪ How do customers find your offering?

▪ How do customers order and purchase the product?

▪ How is your product/service paid for?

▪ How is your product stored?

▪ How is your product moved?

▪ What is the customer really using your product for?

▪ What happens when your product is disposed of?

## Chapter takeaways

▪ Pricing in competitive markets is a clear way of placing or positioning a company in the mind of customers relative to other firms. It indicates whether the brand is up-market or down-market.

▪ Nine forms of positioning by price are listed, including the aspirational position where higher prices helped a brand to turn around.

- Price positioning is dynamic because changes to competitor prices can alter the position.

- To earn higher prices, the chosen positioning must be justified with differentiation. Commodity thinking diminishes the price that can be achieved in the market place. Fortunately there is wide scope for differentiation, functionally, through process and by relationship benefits.

## Management questions for your business

- How does pricing support our company or brand positioning? How does it lend credibility to our differentiation?

- What are the dynamics of our price position – have price or specification changes from competitors changed the relative positioning?

- Is commodity thinking a danger to our business?

- Name a functional benefit important to customers where we can out-perform our competitors over the long term?

- Name a process benefit important to customers where we can out-perform our competitors over the long term?

- Name a relationship benefit important to customers where we can out-perform our competitors over the long term?

- Have we scrutinized the customer sequence from awareness and buying to usage and disposal, to discern new potential benefits we can offer?

## Going further – references and additional reading

Barwise, P. and Meehan, S. (2004) 'Don't be unique, be better', *MIT Sloan Management Review*, Summer.

Bloom, J. (2005) 'Lacoste's Siegel illustrates the sales power of pricing up', *Advertising Age*, 7 February.

*The Economist* (2005) 'Time to put ideas into practice', 23 April.

Fair trade bananas: www.bananalink.org.uk/future/future_2.htm and Prince, R. (2005) 'Savvy Shopper', *Daily Telegraph*, 12 March.

Jones, A. (2004) 'No peace for the market behemoths as unbranded assault continues', *Financial Times*, 21 September.

MacMillan and McGrath (1997) 'Discovering new points of difference', *Harvard Business Review*, August.

Marn, M., Roegner, E. V. and Zawada, C. C. (2004) *The Price Advantage*, Wiley, Hoboken, NJ – see especially Chapter 4.

Rawlinson, R. (1997) 'Suit yourself about designer pricing', *Financial Times*, 4 January.

Sweney, M. (2004) 'Beyond the functional', *Marketing Magazine*, 21 April.

Thomke, S. and von Hippel, E. (2002) 'Customers as innovators – a new way to create value', *Harvard Business Review*, April.

Tyrrell, P. (2004) 'A taste for luxury brings just desserts', *Financial Times*, 26 October.

www.lafarge.com

# 7

# Competing with value players – hit back with benefits

## The value player challenge: cut-price coffins at Costco

**There is no limit** to the markets that discounters are entering. *The Economist* magazine reported that on 16 August 2004, the warehouse-style retailer Costco launched a range of discounted funeral items. Costco's coffins or caskets come in various styles. The 'In God's Care' casket is in 18-gauge steel and is painted Neapolitan blue with silver shading. Normal delivery is within three working days, but the website (www.costco.com) warns that Acts of God can delay delivery beyond these parameters. The real surprise is the price. From a traditional funeral services firm, this coffin would cost $3,500–$5,000. From Costco it is just $924.99 delivered to the funeral parlour of choice. This is a deep discount.

## New threat – deep discount

Brand leaders expect challenger brands to compete at a price somewhere below their own – it is a conventional strategy. For all the reasons, the challenger is obliged to come in a little below the leading brand. But today, deep discounters and disruptive innovators are opening up price chasms:

Aldi
Dell
Easyjet
IKEA
Kwik-save
Lidl
Matalan
Netto
Primark
Ryanair
Superdrug
TK Maxx
Wilkinsons

The value players are on the march. Verdict research published in the *Financial Times* shows that value retailers took a 19.7 percent share of the UK clothing market in 2004 – up 60 percent from 1999. In Germany, hard discounters count their share of the grocery market at 40 percent. Carrefour, the world's second largest retailer, is recording market share losses in its French home market. The gainers are rival Leclerc and hard discounters like Lidl and Aldi. Hard discounters barely existed in France in 1995 with fewer than 200 stores. By 2005, 3,400 hard-discount outlets accounted for 12 percent of the grocery market. With timely relevance, the UK-based Institute of Grocery Distribution chose the impact and growth trends of hard discounters as the theme of their 2004 Global Retailing Conference.

# No room for haughty brand supremacy

Managers always needed to develop a keen sense of the value of their products relative to those of competitors. But now the imperative is stronger, the risks are greater. Lower-priced competitors can severely damage customers' perceptions of value in an industry by encouraging customers to prioritize the search for lower prices rather than any product or service benefits. The old rules of haughty brand superiority are outmoded and new competitive skills are needed.

Faced with a ruthless price-based competitor there seem to be two alternatives:

■ The ostrich approach – continuing with current strategy and hoping the impact will be limited.

■ The rhinoceros approach – going into an attacking charge and fighting back on their ground.

Neither option appears to succeed. Without response, the impact is usually dramatic. Low prices steal customers from existing players and draw in new price-led purchasers, giving scale to the entrant that allows them to increase their market power still further. In the US toy market, the value player is Wal-Mart. In the face of Wal-Mart's price onslaught, retailer KB Toys filed for Chapter 11 bankruptcy protection in 2004 and FAO Schwarz's closed down its chain of toy shops.

The alternative is engaging the rival on price. This price-cutting answer weakens the revenues of the incumbent and confirms, in the eyes of buyers, that the battle is about discounts rather than benefits. Toys R Us fought back against Wal-Mart in the months before Christmas 2004. A report in the *Financial Times* by Lauren Foster (2004) charted the results of the fight-back (as summarized in Table 7.1).

| Table 7.1 | 2004 toy price comparison (USA) |
| --- | --- |

|  | Wal-Mart price | Toys R Us price |
| --- | --- | --- |
| Monopoly (original) | $9.74 | $9.99 |
| FurReal Friend (Luv Cubs) | $34.82 | $29.99 |
| Yard Crew (Big Mike Mowers) | $17.78 | $19.99 |
| Elmo (E L M O) | $24.47 | $29.99 |
| Tonka (mighty dump truck) | $12.96 | $14.99 |

Key: ⬇ indicates lowest price

*Source*: Foster (2004).

Toys R Us, once a discount leader itself, discovered that when a promotional message is founded on low prices, there is nothing left when another retailer consistently undercuts you. Toys R Us considered quitting the toy business early in 2005. Subsequently, the company agreed to be acquired by a private equity consortium, including Bain Capital Partners, Kohlber Kravis Roberts & Co. and Vornado Realty Trust. The attraction is the property portfolio rather than the dwindling share of the toy market.

## Look at the Wal-Mart way and look out!

Let us look at Wal-Mart – the victor in the US toy market and the world leader in opening price chasms for its rivals. A ruthless policy of 'Always low prices. Always' has brought annual sales topping $285 billion in the year to 31 January 2005, representing 11.2 percent growth over the previous year. By 1999, Bentonville-based Wal-Mart had became the world's largest private employer with 1,140,000 associates in ten countries. On the day after Thanksgiving, in November 2002, Wal-Mart sales hit $1.43 billion in one single day. Finally, for a measure of its scale, with annual purchases of $15 billion, Wal-Mart accounted for almost 11 percent of the value of exports from the People's Republic of China in 2003.

How can you defend your market against aggression from the world's largest retailer?

The emergence of no-frills airlines is another example. *McKinsey Quarterly* cites Southwest Airlines, the highly successful low-cost US airline, which increased its share of domestic flight revenue from 3.2 percent in 1990 to 12.9 percent in 2002. Ryanair and EasyJet have seen similar success in Europe. By mid-2005, there were 27 low-cost airlines serving Asia including Air Deccan in India, Air Asia in Malaysia and Tiger Airways in Singapore. All offering cut-price fares.

## Fight back with benefits

Competitors can, however, fight back. Jet Blue – launched in February 2000 in New York – does not offer the lowest fares on the US market, yet succeeds through a benefit-led advertising message to consumers. It trades on such features as its in-flight comforts, 24 channels of DirecTV and industry-leading punctuality. In July 2004, Jet Blue delivered its fourteenth consecutive quarter of profit and a 14.1 percent operating margin.

The answer is neither to cede nor attack on price. Rather it is to identify critical benefits that customers forego with the value player and to build a proposition based on these. Every value player takes away some benefits to fund its price platform. Identify what the customer will miss. Strengthen these benefits and stress their relevance to customers. Fight back on a benefit battlefield.

# Ten strategies to beat the value players

There is, of course, no single strategy to defend against every value player. Each market, customer segment and competitor is different. But there are ten generic approaches that could be considered.

## 1. Innovation, novelty and new products

Low-price operators must make savings in order to give discounts. When these savings are in research and development, to avoid costs or risks of new product failure and the low volumes of new lines, an opportunity is opened for innovation as a differentiator.

*How it works*

The women's clothing chain, Zara, has more than 700 stores in 54 countries. Design is seen as an active innovation process. Every day comments and behaviours from customers are fed back to Arteixo design centre by store staff using handheld communication devices. The 200-strong design team respond and new designs are shipped to stores twice a week. Value-playing competitors may be lower price but they lack the innovation that fashion requires.

A business example is Vacuumschmelze, a leading global manufacturer of advance magnetic materials. This innovative division of Morgan Crucible has a turnover of €300 million and serves customers in watch manufacturing, aviation and retailing, for example with magnetic strips for anti-theft tags. Its lead in process technology was featured in a manufacturing report in the *Financial Times*. Special expertise lies in melting and forming tiny components from nickel, cobalt, silicon and boron. The company's defence against lower-priced products rests in around 1,000 patents.

## 2. Leverage tradition

Value players are frequently new entrants from outside the conventions of an industry. Stelios Haji-Iaonnou, founder of EasyJet, the no-frills airline, had a previous family background in shipping. Coming from the outside can be a strength, but it may also be a vulnerability in an industry where tradition has a value.

### How it works

Long-established companies with emotional historical connections can use this extended credibility to defend against lower-priced competitors. For example, Ravida Sicilian sea salt draws advantage from the fact that the Ravida family have been producing salt in Sicily since 1700.

The history of Heidelberger Drucksmachinen reaches back to Andreas Hamm in 1850 and the manufacture of flat-bed cylinder presses for book printing. Today the company is the world's Number 1 manufacturer of printing presses. The company's advertising highlights the firm's 'passion for print' leveraging its historical tradition.

## 3. Customer responsiveness

Cut-price companies may well save costs by reducing investment in customer support, standardizing ranges or components. They choose to economize on the resources that allow them to respond rapidly to customers' requirements or changing desires.

### How it works

DVDs are on sales from Amazon, all the leading UK grocery supermarkets and even at many petrol filling stations at rock-bottom prices. Yet the UK market leader is HMV, the Top Dog on the UK high street. HMV leads because it is the first to respond to emerging tastes and customer trends. As a new television series is aired, seeking the best situation comedy, HMV is first in promoting candidate DVDs even before customers know they will want them.

Caterpillar is another brand that leverages its knowledge of market needs with responsiveness to individual customers. Its large engine plant at Lafayette, Indiana, produces 11,000 engines per year. These include engines for on and off-road use as well as marine engines. Growth has come from customization. Around 10 percent of the parts can be varied to customer requirements and, as a final production stage, a customized chip can be individually programmed to control important aspects of the engine's operation. Responsiveness is a defence against lower-priced offerings.

## 4. Trust and reassurance

It is often the lesser-known businesses that give the discount prices in an industry. Conveying trust and brand reassurance takes time, consistent strategy and investment in communications. Thus, where there are a number of price-fighting brands, infrequent buyers are often bewildered by the wealth of choice they face. This gives an opportunity to confident brand leaders.

### How it works

In the automotive market, a potential customer could sift through 50 marques, some of which are very competitively priced but are not household names. For a buyer without experience or great interest in car comparisons, there is a short cut: select a known and safe brand. Since 1974, the Volkswagen Golf has been such a safe brand. Its ubiquity is a commendation to the inexpert buyer. On average, 2,100 customers a day bought a Golf between 1974 and 2003. Over a 30-year period, the Golf has been the top-selling model across Europe for most years. The Fiat Punto put it in second place in 1997, as did the Peugeot 206 in 2003. However, in 2004 the Golf led the way again with over 550,000 models sold in Europe.

Similarly, the personal loans market seems like a jungle to the financially unskilled. In the UK, the trust generated by the Lloyds TSB name, is supported by the credentials of being the UK's Number 1 lender for personal loans. Less confident customers will eschew comparison shopping for fear of unknown pitfalls.

Brembo, the Italian manufacturer of high-performance brakes, has achieved an enviable reputation through working with and supplying Motoguzzi and Porsche over the years. Ferrari gave their 2001 'Innovation award' to Brembo, who supply braking systems to the winning Marlboro–Ferrari Formula 1 team. It is readily possible for automotive procurement departments to find lower-priced braking systems. Brembo can charge €350 for a vehicle system. However, more and more engineers are specifying the distinctive bright red Brembo systems for their performance and brand reputation.

## 5. Certainty

With lower-priced products, customers fear that they may be bearing some of the risks. Certainty is a significant reason for them to pay higher prices.

### How it works

In a low-margin industry, airlines need to be price-sensitive buyers. However, their risk aversion is greater than their price sensitivity. GE has crafted a value proposition for leasing the GE90 engine, charged by the hour. However, there is a nuance that makes all the difference to customers. Nagle and Cressman (2002) explain that the price is for uptime and removes uncertainties of time-consequences of scheduled and unscheduled maintenance.

## 6. Expertise

Many low-cost operations fund their competitiveness by stripping out personal guidance to customers. Turn this to advantage when facing value players and highlight the level of support available.

### How it works

In the UK, certain retailers stand out above others for their service and particularly, the knowledge levels or expertise of their staff. One of these is Waitrose, growing profitably in one of the world's most competitive grocery markets. Leaders Tesco and Asda rival each other in price claims, and low-end operators like Lidl, Kwiksave and Aldi come in below them. Yet upmarket Waitrose goes from strength to strength. The secret? Waitrose combines the convenience of a supermarket with the expertise and service of a specialist shop (see Figure 7.1).

## The Peculiar Incident of the Fishmonger Performing on Hilary's Kitchen Table

When Hilary Stuart decided to invite some close friends round for supper, she wanted to cook them something special. A few days later she saw just the thing in a magazine - Gratin of Plaice Fillets.

Although the recipe seemed straightforward, it stressed that the plaice fillets must have their skins removed. Thinking this might be rather tricky, she called the supermarket where she always bought her fish. No problem they said. They'd be happy to skin them - all she had to do was pick them up.

In the afternoon before the supper, Hilary's husband - who will now be known as 'The Stupid Fool' - was dispatched to the supermarket to pick up a few last-minute items and, of course, the eight skinned plaice fillets.

The 'Stupid Fool' returned with - you've guessed it - eight plaice fillets that hadn't been skinned. While he burbled excuses, Hilary took decisive action and rang the supermarket.

Rather than you come to us again, they said, we'll come to you. And they did. 30 minutes later their fishmonger arrived.

Opening his set of knives, he proceeded to expertly skin the fillets there and then on Hilary's kitchen table.

So Hilary was able to cook the supper she'd intended and her friends were very complimentary.

Even 'The Stupid Fool' had an enjoyable evening, despite receiving the occasional withering look from Hilary.

The above incident was recounted by a customer of our Wallingford branch.

**Figure 7.1** Waitrose advertisement
Supplied and reproduced with permission.

Furthermore, staff are not employees but partners. As co-owners, they have a higher level of commitment to customer service – many will have worked for the business longer than 20 years. For example, Waitrose was the first UK supermarket to employ a Master of Wine, Julian Brind, who has worked at Waitrose since 1971.

Bookselling has become highly competitive, with websites and supermarkets under-cutting traditional bookstores. Yet Waterstones, located in high streets around the UK, continues to thrive. All the staff are capable of answering or guiding customers, with a depth of knowledge and a love of books. You can rely on the staff recommendations handwritten on shelf cards. In April 2005, Waterstones was named as Bookselling Company of the Year at the British Book Trade Awards.

## 7. Range, choice and selection

Discounters frequently provide standard ranges at very low prices. For example, hard discounter Aldi has 7,000 stores and is close to being one of the world's top ten largest food retailers. Yet it offers only 700 different high-volume products. The very narrowness of the range and the inevitable standardization provides an opportunity for creative rivals.

### How it works

The USA retailer, Target, based in Minneapolis, attacks Wal-Mart with an edited up-market selection of goods. Some of these are created exclusively by its own design team. *The Economist* magazine commented that such is the status of these designs that some customers affectionately nickname Target as 'tar-jay' affecting a French pronunciation to highlight design flair.

## 8. Personalization, customer insight

The discount model piles it high, sells it cheap and often operates with high levels of automation and low staffing support. It is a standard model that offers little personal treatment. Consequently, relevant and personalized information can defeat lower prices.

*How it works*

The UK grocery retailer, Waitrose, has a section on its website listing recipes of all types and extends this service with a personalization option – customers are able to create their own folder of 'My favourite recipes', saving recipes for easy subsequent access.

A business example comes from the renal division of Baxter UK. Writing in *Sloan Management Review*, Sandra Vandermerwe (2000) describes how the company sold disposable bags for home kidney dialysis. As well as facing lower-priced competitors for peritoneal dialysis, customers were able to remove toxic waste from their blood using hemodialysis products which were cheaper on a bag-for-bag basis. Baxter used customer insight to map the treatment activities. As a result of this relevant knowledge, they focused on adding value by helping patients to update prescriptions, maintain machines and dispose of used dialysis bags. This personalized customer education and support kept patients at home longer and hence increased bag sales for Baxter.

## 9. Time-based understanding

Value players offer an obvious trade-off to customers – saving money versus saving time. They frequently use the customer to provide some of their own services. The original self-service supermarkets handed over the task of produce selection to customers and saved staff. IKEA expect customers to make their own choice, locate the flatpack in the warehouse area before the checkout, carry out their own deliveries and assemble the kits to complete the furniture. The company has trans-ferred the time-consuming aspects to the customer. The opportunity is then to serve time-constrained customer segments.

*How it works*

In a cash-rich, time-poor society, this trade off can be a profitable approach for a brand battling with a value player. *McKinsey Quarterly* Frank, George and Narasimhan (2004) tell how, in the USA, the drugstore Walgreens has deliberately located its stores on corners with easy parking, and has conceived time-saving strategies for its customers. For example, it offers an on-line or telephone pre-ordering system for prescriptions with a drive-through collection point. Despite the price-led pressure of Wal-Mart and others, Walgreens has achieved double-digit same-store sales growth since 1999.

## 10. Add services

The discounter can tempt customers with low prices by cutting out services. An example is Lidl, one of the top ten food retailers in Germany, which has a philosophy that you only pay for what you get. This means that customers pay for carrier bags, have no shopping baskets on offer and must pay a deposit for trolleys. If the discounters strip out service, the competitive answer is to add differentiating services.

*How it works*

Porsche is the leading motor industry brand by margin, earning a higher return per vehicle than any other marque. In the face of lower-cost sports cars from other respected car companies, what benefits could Porsche offer to secure the loyalty of their drivers? Understanding emotional anxieties can uncover opportunities for profitable solutions and provide a weapon against cheaper rivals. Research identified that a significant proportion of Porsche owners travel extensively on business flights. Their insight is, that to the owner, their Porsche is like a prized jewel. You do not leave prized jewels in open-air parking lots at airports! So Porsche came to an agreement with Avis that certain owners could leave their cars safely under cover in the Avis premises. It is a good proposition for Avis who can promote rental cars at the destination airport. And it also supports the Porsche buyers' perception that they have bought a premium brand.

The printing press manufacturer, Heidelberger Druckmaschinen has set up the Heidleberger Print Media Academy (PMA). Bernd Schopp, Head of PMA said 'The Print Media Academy has made it its job to give managers and employees from the print media industry the knowledge they need to successfully compete on future markets', summarizing the aims of the PMA. Tailor-made programmes cover practical product training for prepress, press and postpress for customers and potential customers. Service sustains its Number 1 position in the market.

It is essential to understand all the benefits that may be relevant to customers and focus attention on the appealing benefits that customers forego when they buy from the lowest-price supplier. In the final analysis, prices in some categories may need to be trimmed. The premium price you can command may be reduced, but some level of premium needs to be upheld.

## You cannot hold all the business

One conclusion is clear – in the face of new and low-cost competitors, a company can utilize some of these strategies, but will not be able to retain all the business. Invariably, some price-sensitive customers will defect to the newcomer.

The consulting firm, McKinsey, investigated incumbent strategies in deregulated industries, publishing their findings in an article, 'The race to the bottom', by Florissen, Mauer, Schmidt and Vahlkamp. They report that managers in newly deregulated industries often over-react. Typically they make four mistakes:

- ▦ focusing on the lowest priced competitor rather than the one that is best known in the market and most likely to lure customers away;

- ▦ over-estimating switching rates in the face of low-price competition. In fact comparatively few customers actually switch unless the enormity of the price differential outweighs the inconvenience of changing providers. The analysis shows that incumbents charging a 5 percent premium experience a switching rate of below 2 percent of customers per year;

- ▦ failing to consider the value of different types of customers – some are less valuable being willing to switch and others have high value being open to cross-selling. It is more profitable to lose fickle customers than to try to keep them by lowering prices to all customers;

- ▦ failing to evaluate the true cost of serving individual customers. Without distinguishing costs by customer type, there is a danger that average pricing may lead to prices below costs for some customers.

Finally they recommend that incumbents must maintain a premium and be prepared to shed a tranche of customers to low-priced competitors. In these circumstances, to optimize value it is necessary to lose customers. You cannot keep them all.

## Chapter takeaways

- Brand leaders expect challengers to undercut them. But today's hard-discount competitors are having a greater impact.

- Matching prices brings down industry and company profits.

- The better response is to focus on benefits that the discounters strip away. Ten approaches are suggested to protect a premium price.

- Prices may need to be trimmed to continue to deliver value, but some level of premium should be defended with benefits. Ultimately, some price-sensitive customers will be lost but allowing this will preserve value in the market.

## Management questions for your business

- How might value players disrupt our market in the future?

- Which benefits would discounters chose to strip away?

- How could we respond with enhanced benefits?

- Which customers are likely to react favourably to benefit propositions?

- Are we over-estimating the potential costs and levels of defection in the face of low-priced competitors?

- Does our pricing strategy maintain our premium until actual trigger levels of defection are reached?

- Should we review the level of our price premium?

# Going further – references and additional reading

*The Economist* (2004) 'Special report: Wal-Mart', 17 April.

*The Economist* (2004) 'Stiff competition', 21 August.

Ewing, J. (2004) 'How far can Germany's Aldi go?', *Business Week*, 26 April.

Florissen, A., Mauer, B., Schmidt, B., and Vahlkamp, T. (2001) 'The race to the bottom', *McKinsey Quarterly*, 3.

Foster, L. (2004) 'Toys' sad story', *Financial Times*, 17 September.

Frank, R. J., George, J. P., and Narasimhan, L. (2004) 'When your competitor delivers more for less', *McKinsey Quarterly*, 1.

March, P. (2001) 'How to fight off your competitors', *Financial Times*, 2 August – a number of industrial examples are drawn from this article.

Nagle, T. and Cressman, G. E. (2002) 'Don't just set prices, manage them', *Marketing Management*, November/December.

Tassell, T. (2005) quotes Verdict Research in 'Primark dressed for success without cutting corners', *Financial Times*, 16 July.

Vandermerwe, S. (2000) 'How increasing value to customers improves business results', *Sloan Management Review*, Fall.

www.igd.com – Institute of Grocery Distribution

www.jetblue.com

# What is a price war, where do they happen?

A price war occurs where one competitor in a market significantly undercuts the prices which leads to a cycle of one or more competitors lowering their prices in order to undercut each other. The objective is normally to gain commercial advantage, and the result is usually heavy 'casualties' on all sides.

Professor Michael Porter (2004) identified in his book, *Competitive Advantage*, the industry characteristics leading to intense levels of rivalry between firms that threaten industry profits. This is the context for potential price wars. These characteristics are listed below:

■ Industries with a large number of firms, particularly if they have similar market shares and ambitions to gain leadership over rivals.

■ Industries facing slowing market growth. For example in China car sales grew 60–70 percent in 2002 and similarly in 2003, slowing to 16 percent in 2004 and further to just 5–10 percent in 2005. The consequence was a price war, with the price of the Honda Accord and the Ford Mondeo dropping 10 percent in 2005 to below the 200,000 yuan level.

■ High fixed costs, resulting in a battle for scale to cover these costs. For hotels staff costs and asset overheads are significantly more than the variable costs associated with each guest. Winning one more guest from a rival hotel makes a significant profit impact.

■ High storage costs or perishable products. Airline seats are an example of perishable products – once the plane takes off the seat cannot be sold.

■ Low switching costs for customers, making it attractive to sellers to try to gain rapid share through cutting prices, which competitors must match to retain business.

■ Low levels of product differentiation. For example, most car drivers believe brands of petrol are interchangeable.

■ Strategic stakes are high. If a firm believes its position is threatened or that it can overturn existing market leadership, price responses are attractive. The battle in India for broadband subscribers between attacker Bharti and the state-owned companies of Bharat Sanchar Nigam Ltd and Mahanagar Telephone Nigam Ltd is an illustration of high strategic stakes.

- High exit barriers, where a firm is unable to find alternative uses for capacity or skills as a market declines.

- Diversity of rivals, with competitors operating to different rules or cultures. The market for music CDs is an example, where specialist retailers compete with supermarkets and international web businesses and even downloading alternatives.

- Industry shakeouts, where the market size and available business is insufficient to provide a profitable return for all the firms competing in that market place and price wars force out weaker players. This may be occurring in the deregulated market for UK telephone number enquiries.

The following is a price risk checklist. How does your industry score?

- Large number of firms?
- Slowing market growth?
- High fixed costs?
- High storage costs/perishable products?
- Low switching costs?
- Little product differentiation?
- High strategic stakes?
- High exit barriers?
- Diversity of rivals?
- Industry shakeouts?

The above are the industry conditions most likely to lead to price wars, though they may occur in almost any market or industry.

# Does a price war make sense?

There are three circumstances where it may make sense to launch a price assault:

Reason 1. Customer opportunity – some markets have significant latent demand at lower prices. There may be many consumers willing to buy when prices drop to an affordable trigger level. A company matching this required price wins rapid volume growth. This scale advantage from high market share permits it to progress down the experience curve faster than competitors and thereby gain long-term cost advantage. This is a penetration pricing strategy. In the UK, the introduction of the 1830 Beer Act created a new type of public house. Within six months, nearly 25,000 new beer houses had sprung up. The latent demand for beer led to a price war and beer sales increased for the successful brewers. More recent examples of success in penetration pricing are in the calculator and computer keyboard markets.

Reason 2. Competitive opportunity – if there are significant volume and profit available at a lower price *and* there are non-cost reasons why your competitor cannot follow. This might occur where a minor player cuts prices to take the share away from a major player whose response is constrained. The big firm cannot cut prices in one area without the discount leaking to all areas of its operation.

Reason 3. Company cost advantage – if you have a significant and sustainable cost advantage over rivals, then it is an option to take market share using price. Significant cost advantage is defined by Marn, Roeger and Zawada (2004) as at least 30 percent lower costs. Dell and Wal-Mart are firms that have used their low-cost business models in this way.

There are reasons when it is profitable to launch a price war, as listed:

*Customer reason*: significant latent demand at lower prices.

*Competitive reason*: market situation where the competitor cannot follow you.

*Company reason*: substantial cost advantage over rivals.

The bottom line is that there are some occasions when a low-cost assault on a market can tap latent value. In these circumstances the low price is a means of unlocking and capturing this value. In practice, these occasions are rare.

## Volume increases rarely match the original profit foregone

A small price reduction has a disproportionate impact on profit.

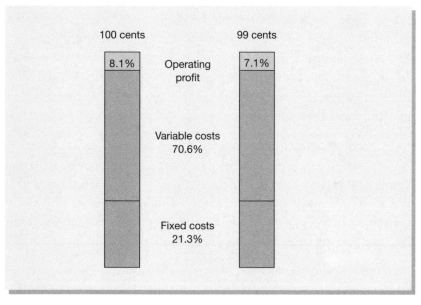

**Figure 8.2**    The cost of a price cut. For a typical firm, with average variable and fixed costs, a price cut of 1 percent from 100 cents to 99 cents, reduces profit by 12.3 percent.

With a straightforward price cut of 5 percent, typically an increase in volume of 18–20 percent is needed to recover operating profit. And remember that a sudden expansion in volume will have ramifications for the variable costs of warehousing, inventory and delivery, let alone advertising costs to communicate the cut. Volume surges on this scale are implausible. Most price wars simply pass value from producers to customers and do not capture value for the producer.

After a bruising price war in the Indian detergent market in 2004, Hindustan Lever Limited (HLL), the Indian arm of Unilever, extended the war to shampoos with a 'one plus one free' offer on Clinic Plus and Sunsilk brands. Rival Procter & Gamble denied that it would join this price war, but two weeks later cut prices on Pantene and Head & Shoulders shampoos. Mr Mukal Deoras, then Category Head of Haircare at HLL accepted that the decision would hit margins. He was quoted on the Hindu Business Line as saying, 'The answer is how do we neutralise this loss. We believe a recovery will happen through volume increase. The driver of profit growth is going to be volumes.' A few weeks after this interview, Mr Deoras left HLL for a new role in Colgate. In February 2005 HLL announced its fourth consecutive quarterly fall in profit.

## Any advantage is short-lived

Joel Urbany (2001) investigated managers' beliefs that buying market share through aggressive short-term pricing leads to permanent increases in profitability. His findings were that price cuts were quickly matched. Any gain in share is short-lived and industry profits may end up falling.

If there is success in attracting new customers through price alone, competitors will simply follow and neutralize the gains. In the US mutual fund companies the three biggest players are Vanguard Group, Capital Group and Fidelity Investments. Vanguard has long trumpeted its advantage in low-fee investing. In August 2004, Fidelity responded by cutting fees on five of its index funds. A month later, Capital Group followed by announcing two 5 percent across the board fee cuts. Early in 2005, John Brennan, chairman of Vanguard, dismissed the Fidelity cuts as a 'marketing ploy'. Fidelity responded by making the cuts permanent and, in April 2005, Vanguard lowered the barrier for access to the extra-low fee share classes of its funds. If an action has an impact, a reaction will follow.

## And customers get the wrong message

A further damaging consequence of a price war is the implied communication to customers. Promoting price cuts simply recommends to
buyers that they should select on price alone and disregard benefits.
The price war among Dutch supermarkets in 2003 sensitized customers
to seek out further discount offers. Chinese car buyers, who had
seen prices drop steadily over 18 months from 2003 levels, astutely
delayed their purchases through 2005 in anticipation of further
reductions.

Price wars can also flag up memorably low prices for familiar products.
Seeing CDs on sale at £9.99 in UK supermarkets imprinted a value
threshold in customers' minds. Prices tend to be inflexible upwards and
any price increase returning to 'normal' level is perceived as making the
products 'expensive'. This can inhibit future demand.

## Strategic shakeouts don't happen

The analogy of 'War' implies a decisive battle between two armies where
one defeats and destroys the other. The allusion is unhelpful, since the
norm is for the battle to drag into a long and painful war of attrition.
One side rarely defeats the other. Normally both sides lose resources and
damage industry credibility and reputation.

In 1993, Rupert Murdoch started a price war in the UK broadsheet
market, slashing the cover price of *The Times* to knock out the *Daily
Telegraph*. The *Telegraph* responded with a discounted subscription offer
to secure the loyalty of its readers, and survived. The sales of *The Times*
increased but profit was elusive. The prices of the broadsheets remained
needlessly low throughout the 1990s starving the newspapers of
resources and inhibiting readers' perceptions of value in this market.
No-one won the battle – everyone lost. Shakeouts don't happen.

Another industry where shakeouts have not occurred is aviation. In the
USA, the Air Transport Association has recorded more than 100
bankruptcies since deregulation in 1988, including the once proud Pan
Am who led the way with trans-Atlantic flights and the jumbo-jet. Yet

whenever an airline goes bust, someone buys the planes and plans ways to put them back into the sky again. Warren Buffet has acidly observed that airlines as a whole have not netted a dime since 1903. Price wars have destroyed value for 100 years.

The following list summarizes what is wrong with price wars:

■ Volume will not compensate for lost margin.

■ Price advantages are normally short-lived.

■ Distorts customer expectations.

■ Sets lower reference prices.

■ Strategic shakeouts don't happen.

■ Industry value is destroyed.

Price wars are almost invariably destructive of value, inhibit industry growth and reputation, and often damage the careers of the individuals taking part.

## How price wars really start

Contrary to management opinion, most price wars are not strategic exploitation of market growth potential or cost advantage. Most begin where one competitor misinterprets a competitor's actions or acts and fails to consider the likely response of rivals. The price war may start when Company A cuts prices in one city to clear obsolete stock and Company B sees this as an industry-wide price assault and responds aggressively. Both will believe the other started the war.

The 2002 tabloid newspaper price war in the UK began when the *Daily Star* cut its cover price to 10p to increase readership. The *Daily Mirror* saw the opportunity to encourage its infrequent readers to buy it every day and slashed its price to 20p. The market's leading tabloid, the *Sun*, interpreted the move as a direct attack on its position and retaliated with price cuts. The cost to all the tabloids was huge.

Alternatively, a price war may start when one party launches a new and superior product that causes the market to reappraise existing brands.

Other parties may be compelled to reduce the price of current models lest sales are lost to the new product. Under-pricing new products can inadvertently set off price wars.

## Avoid, avoid, avoid

To capture value and deliver optimal profits, the answer is to avoid price wars if at all possible. How do you stop price wars before they start? There are some clear strategies.

First, focus public communications on value delivery and benefits rather than price. Take the debate away from the orange starburst. Build the reputation of the industry among all consumers to encourage competitors to join you on the high ground. The UK grocer, Waitrose, has consistently used high-standard photography to imbue its products with a sense of quality. Its prices are generally competitive, but all communication is focused on benefits.

Second, companies, particularly leaders in the market, are advised to make their strategic intentions clear, so that rivals understand their actions. Prevent misinterpretation. Direct communication to competitors may be illegal or inappropriate, but speaking at industry events or communicating to trade journalists is perfectly acceptable. Clarify that promotions to clear surplus stock are just that and not part of a price-cutting agenda. Imply the benefits of low-cost production as a potential deterrent to price-cutters.

The public strategic statement that 'We will match market prices', sounds as if it is inviting a price war. Thinking behind the rhetoric, the opposite is actually true. The message is decoded by competitors. They understand that any price reduction will be replicated, which means a price-cutting strategy will gain no competitive advantage. Result: competition focus on benefit selling.

Third, consider the implications for competitors of new product launches, product repositioning and campaigns. Obviously the intention is to win a larger share of the market and this should be planned over the long term. Progressive market share gains, earned over the duration, are often accepted more readily. Sudden hikes in sales at a competitor's expense all too often provoke retaliation.

Fourth, do not over-react to apparent signs of price activity from rivals. Check and corroborate all the facts. Reflect on the consequences before making any riposte.

In summary, four strategies help avoid price wars:

1  Communicate benefits rather than price.

2  Make strategic intentions clear.

3  Consider how competitors will react to new products.

4  Check the facts before responding to competitors' price activity.

If the facts are checked and a competitor has initiated hostile price activity, there are four options for consideration.

1  Do nothing: the action may be temporary, it may affect you less than the competitor hopes and reaction by you may encourage the competitor to go further.

2  React with a non-price response.

3  React with a creative price response.

4  Match the price cut head-on.

The first three options should be evaluated and exhausted before you join the fray. If a response is needed the non-price answer can be more effective.

# Kick 'em with non-price responses

Rao, Bergen and Davis (2000) have suggested four types of non-price action that might be taken

1  Focus on quality not price. Their example is the Ritz-Carlton hotel in Kuala Lumpur. In 1997 the Malaysian business economy was in disarray and Indonesian forest fires were jeopardizing tourism, leading to a collapse in hotel demand. Rival hotels responded by dropping room rates and economized on flowers and other luxury

touches. The Ritz-Carlton chose to emphasize quality over price, meeting flight arrivals with flowers and music, providing new services such as a 'laptop doctor' to deal with guests' IT difficulties. Ritz-Carlton was the long-run victor.

2   Alerting customers to risk. Insurance companies often point to their speedy claims service as a reminder to buyers that a lower-priced policy may not respond as rapidly. Elsewhere IBM and Fedex have both used communication messages of security and stability to appeal to risk averse customers, reminding them of the potential consequences of shortfall from cheap rivals. A non-price response might highlight the performance risks of lower-priced products in marketing promotions.

3   Emphasize other negative consequences. Rexam, the leader in packaging and StoraEnso, the paper company, both use their environmental credentials as a means of protecting themselves and their customers. The implicit thought is that customers could face adverse publicity if they were to use suppliers without such concern for the future of the planet.

4   Seek support from other contributors. In the USA and elsewhere, industries fearing price wars from imported products have rushed to their government for protection, seeking tariff barriers to give them time to defend themselves. Distributors may be able to support a favoured brand during a price war by ensuring availability and recommendation.

## Fear and emotion to fight price cuts

Visual imagery can help. During a price war following electricity supply deregulation, one of the low-price combatants, Independent Energy, went bankrupt. The incumbent ran full-page advertisements warning all electricity users of the dangers of choosing low-price newcomers who could go bust. The image of the lights going out was sombre.

Emotional connections can be used. In the face of lower prices from rivals, it is tempting to join the fray and drop prices to match. Suzy Bashford (2004), writing in *Marketing Magazine*, identified 'Buy one

get one free' (BOGOF) deals in UK grocery stores on 12 of the most presti-
gious brands, including Lynx, Timotei, Johnson & Johnson and Bird's
Eye. By contrast, in the same grocery stores, Heinz ran an attention
gaining 'Win a Home' promotion with an instant-win prize linked to the
homely values of the Heinz brand. The detergent brand Aerial, which has
built a long-term association with tennis, sponsors 2004 quarter-finalist
Tim Henman and provided an on-pack promotion offering free tennis
lessons during the Wimbledon tournament. Emotional images of home
and sporting success were effective non-price answers.

## Be creative and selective in your responses

Companies can try to defuse price competition by smart price responses.
Challenged by a price-cutting competitor, a brand might pre-empt the
price war by offering a stock-loading promotion to large customers. This
brings forward future orders and customers are therefore not in the
market when the rival slashes prices. The price cut fails to deliver the
expected volume uptake and the competitor learns a lesson about the
non-viability of price wars.

If it is impossible for a company to escape a price war, it should limit its
responses to the channel, region or segment where competition is most
threatening. Tesco, the UK retailer, focuses price cuts on products that
tend to be bought primarily by price-sensitive shoppers. Instead of
discounting bananas, which are bought by all shoppers, it may cut the
price of its 'Value' brand margarine, bought by price-conscious shoppers
and few others.

Narrowing the price response to certain pack sizes works – there is no
need to drop the price of an entire range if your customer understanding
says that price-sensitive shoppers always buy the jumbo box. Again, the
price response can be restricted to one channel, one country, one time
of day.

A fighting brand can be introduced. This can be priced competitively to
fight the price-cutters head-on, without impacting on the brand
reputation of the major brand. The airline KLM introduced Buzz, its
own no-frills airline, to compete with EasyJet and Ryanair.

The more selective the response is the less the damage to profits and brand reputation.

# If you have to fight, punch hard, once

Sometimes a price war cannot be avoided. For example, when a predatory competitor challenges the core business. An Internet auction is effectively a price war in a technological context. A buying company provides a specification and invites potential sellers to bid against each other in a real-time Internet auction. This has all the characteristics of a price war, and if there is no other way to gain business, it must be endured.

When all other options have been exhausted, direct head-on competition in a price war is the last resort. In these circumstances, the recommendation is to fight hard. This means getting to the bottom fast. Salami-slicing prices in an ongoing downward spiral simply teaches customers to hold on for even lower prices next month. Getting to the bottom fast discourages the competitor and speeds the end of the price war. The aim must be to restore normality as rapidly as possible.

# Retreating may be the most profitable strategy

Fighting may not be the only option. Price wars take time, management focus and money resource. There is a further radical approach. Perhaps you do not fight, but you cede the market to value players and build new businesses via innovation and opportunity evaluation.

The diversified technology company 3M has made a virtue of inventing new products and markets. Speaking at the annual meeting of stockholders in May 2005, the Chief Executive Officer of 3M, James McNerney, highlighted innovation as one the company's 'pillars of growth' with opportunities in track and trace, nanotechnology, separation and filtration, and sensors and diagnostics. As older products like videotape became commoditized, it cedes these businesses to low-priced competitors and focuses on the new. For financial year 2004, sales revenues rose 9.8 percent and net income by 24 percent.

Hochtief, the German-based international construction services provider, took exactly this track. In the 1980s, Hochtief was one of the leading building firms in Germany. It participated fully in the rebuilding bonanza following German reunification, constructing the Congress Centre in Weimar and the new Israeli Embassy in Berlin. The end of this boom came in 1995 and since then German building output has halved, with three-quarters of workers losing their jobs. The business decline caused a price war with serious consequences: Hochtief's biggest rival, Phillip Holzmann, went bankrupt in 2002, despite a government-backed rescue attempt. Walter Bau, the third largest German building firm, became insolvent in 2005. Yet Hochtief avoided this disaster and thrived by moving out of its heartland. In 1995, its culture, history and four-fifths of its business were in Germany. By 2005, four-fifths of its business were *outside* Germany. Hochtief ceded domestic contracts to rivals and embraced an international strategy, buying Turner, a large US builder, in 1999 and moving into facilities management. For example, Hochtief designed, financed, built and operates Athens airport. This expertise has lead to the company operating airports in Sydney, Dusseldorf, Hamburg and Tirana.

If there is no value available in your market, move on to where profits can be made.

## Prepare now

Finally, price wars are an unattractive feature of twenty-first-century business life. They happen and will continue to occur. Managers must be ready and prepared. Talk to people who were involved in previous price wars. Learn the skills and emotions. Establish contingency plans lest a competitor launch an inescapable war.

Put all the deterrent strategies in place . . . and hope.

# Chapter takeaways

- Price wars occur when one competitor significantly undercuts prevailing prices and others respond. They may occur in any market but are particularly likely in industries with pressures such as slowing growth, high fixed costs and low levels of differentiation.

- Price assaults can make sense only in a small number of situations where significant latent demand exists and competitor responses are constrained.

- In most situations price wars destroy value. Volume increases do not achieve expectations, competitors match prices and customers learn to buy on price.

- Price wars normally begin through misinterpretation and over-reaction.

- Recommended strategies are:
  - Take actions to stop price wars before they start.
  - Answer with non-price response.
  - React with creative or selective price responses. If you must participate, fight hard and abbreviate the war.
  - Consider ceding the market and moving to better sources of value.

# Management questions for your business

- How likely is a price war in our market?
- Is there latent demand at lower prices to attract a price-based competitor?
- How low are our costs compared with rivals?
- Do our communications and actions deter price competitors?
- Can we be sure our actions will not trigger a price war in error?

- Do we corroborate rumours of competitor price activity before reacting?
- Who are the potential aggressors, what will their approach be and how might we respond?
- Are our managers prepared for a price war?

# Going further – references and additional reading

Bashford, S. (2004) 'Price promotion: the brand killer', *Marketing Magazine*, 30 June.

Chatterjee, P. (2004) 'Price war bruises HLL Margins', *Hindu Business Line*, 16 April.

Currier, C. (2005) 'Investing: Big Guns in Price War', *International Herald Tribune*, 23 April.

*Hindustan Times*, 'Hindustan Lever Q4 net falls', 11 February.

Humby, C. and Hunt, T., with Phillips, T. (2003) *Scoring Points – How Tesco is winning customer loyalty*, Kogan Page, London.

Marn, M., Roegner, E. V. and Zawada, C. C. (2004) *The Price Advantage*, Wiley, Hoboken, NJ – see Chapter 9 'Price wars'.

Milne, R. (2005) 'Hochtief builds far from home', *Financial Times*, 11 May.

Netflix case study researched using www.netflix.com, www.blockbuster.com, www.walmart.com and the Motley Fool website www.fool.com commentary by Rick Aristotle Munarriz.

Porter, M. E. (2004) *Competitive Advantage, Techniques for Analysing Industries and Competitors*, The Free Press, New York, NY.

Rao, A. R., Bergen, M. E. and Davis, S. (2000) 'How to fight a price war', *Harvard Business Review*, March/April.

*Times of India* (2005) 'Bharti has reduced tariffs for broadband service', 7 May.

Urbany, J. E. (2001) 'Are your prices too low?', *Harvard Business Review*, October.

# 3

# Company success: smarter ways to capture value

# 9

# Fixing the right price – structures, segments and stairways

## Fixing the prices of new cars – best and worst practice

**In August 1959,** the British Motor Corporation launched the most exciting car of its time. The magazine *Autocar* selected the Mini as its 'Car of the Twentieth Century'. Alex Issigonis had designed an astonishingly space efficient vehicle – the transverse engine mounting allowed 80 percent of the car's length to be devoted to passenger accommodation. The style had a classless appeal to motorists of all ages. The advertising promised, 'The car of the future – now.' The magazine *Autosport* reviewed the car under the headline, 'BMC's new baby' and its car reviewer placed an order himself.

Yet BMC lost its nerve on the eve of the launch, reducing the planned list price by £50 to £496, just below £500 – the level of perceived psychological importance. The car was a sales success and demand outstripped supply. Ford Motor Company bought a Mini and reverse engineered the design, concluding that it was being sold at a loss. Lack of profit meant that BMC could not invest in the car's subsequent development. The Mark II, with the wind-up windows that drivers demanded, did not appear until 1967.

Mercedes avoided the same error 40 years later. The planned price of its A-class model was DM29,500, just below the supposedly important DM30,000 barrier. They consulted Kucher and Partners, a Bonn-based firm specializing in pricing strategies. After detailed

▶

consumer research, Mercedes found that the 25 percent of buyers
who would be likely to buy the A-class valued its features strongly.
The research supported a launch at DM31,000. Sales soon hit their
targets in Germany – and Mercedes made an extra DM300 million a
year.

*Source*: Lester (2002).

## How could we set the price?

There is a spectrum of price-setting mechanisms from auction to price
list which includes

- auction, reverse auction
- bi-lateral bargaining
- dynamic pricing
- fixed price list.

The auction is a mechanism where prospective customers bid for
products until one outbids the others. The Dutch auction, or reverse
auction, is another form. Here a lot is offered at a high price, which then
drops by steps until a buyer bids successfully. The first bidder secures the
lot in this model. Bi-lateral bargaining or haggling is another price-
setting model. These first-degree discrimination approaches are
individual, time-consuming and effort intensive.

With Internet-enabled dynamic pricing, buyers or groups of buyers
make binding bids which suppliers can accept or decline. In effect this
system lets customers collectively decide what they are willing to pay for
goods or services. Scott McNealy (2001), CEO of Sun Microsystems,
forecast in the *Harvard Business Review* that the dynamic pricing model
is the future form. Yet today's prevailing approach is the fixed price list.
Even Sun Microsystems currently has a fixed price list because this is the
model of choice for most buyers. It can, of course, be over-laid with
discount scales for second-degree discrimination and tailored by
segment as third-degree discrimination.

So, for most companies a fixed price will be set.

Setting the right price is crucial. A 2003 study by Michael Marn, Eric Roegner and Craig Zawada found that 80–90 percent of all poorly chosen prices were too low. Where the price is incorrect, most times it will be wrong by being under-priced. Charging too little foregoes revenues and profits that could be reinvested. It also positions the product at a lower level in the market. This chapter looks at setting the smart price.

There is a three-stage process to getting the price exactly right: considering customers, considering competitors and considering company objectives and aspirations. *Ashridge*'s Steve Watson (2003), author of 'The long and the short of pricing', expressed it lucidly: 'Pricing decisions are made where the key pricing forces meet. This is the interface between the three main players: the buyer, the seller and the competitor.' It is an iterative process, informed by pricing research, pricing experience and good judgement for the future.

## Stage 1. Customer factors

Calculate the value to the customer, calibrating the benefits provided by the goods or the service. For example, a company clearly understands the value an agent brings in representing them in the market and normally offers a fixed percentage of the turnover he introduces to the principal. Different customer groups may gain value from the product or service differently and so present opportunities for discriminatory pricing structures or segmentation in order to capture the available value.

You consider ability to pay. Can the customer afford the product or service? There may be a need and it may represent good value, but it is important to ensure that the customer has the cash flow or funds available to make the transaction. Again, different customer groups may have differential ability to pay. If different customer groups value the product differently, there may be opportunities for price discrimination. Ensure there will not be a negative impact on one market through leakage from another.

Then you establish willingness to pay. Are there any existing reference price levels in the market or in the mind of the customer? What price has been charged previously by yourself or by an alternative supplier? Is the alternative a directly comparable product? How convenient and accessible is the alternative?

## Audi, BMW, Mercedes cannot capture all the value

**The UK authority** on second-hand car prices, *Glass's Guide*, confirms that the colour of a car increases or reduces its value. Two identical specification cars will be worth different amounts dependent on colour. The *Daily Telegraph* quoted prices for upper-medium prestige cars, like Audi A4s, BMW 3 series and Mercedes C-class after one year and 12,000 miles:

| | |
|---|---|
| Metallic black | Top price |
| Metallic silver | £200 reduction |
| Metallic blue | £450 reduction |
| Flat black | £700 reduction |
| Metallic red | £1,200 reduction |
| Metallic green | £1,200 reduction |
| Flat red | £1,700 reduction |
| Metallic gold | £1,950 reduction |
| Metallic purple | £1,950 reduction |
| Flat blue | £1,950 reduction |
| Flat white | £2,700 reduction |

Do car buyers value one colour over another? Yes – as demonstrated by the above figures.

Can car buyers afford to pay colour price premium? Again the answer is yes.

It is the third question that constrains the car manufacturers from capturing value. Are new car buyers willing to pay a different price for each colour, a price that reflects the colour's perceived value? Answer no. While, metallic painting is seen as a more expensive process (and therefore carries a premium), within paint type, colour is not seen as an acceptable reason for a premium price. Car manufacturers are unable to capture this value.

These three factors will identify a potential price or range of prices that match the customer analysis.

## Stage 2. Competitive factors

Consider the impact this price may have on competitors? Will it compel them into pricing action? Does it create opportunities for them? Will it start a price war? Does the proposed price accord with current pricing assumptions in the market or is it a departure that may cause competitors to revise their own plans?

Beyond competitor responses, the potential price must be reviewed for reactions it may prompt from other bodies. Are there any stakeholders who have an interest in pricing? Government may interpret pricing that leads to unusually high margins, as an opportunity for a windfall tax. This has occurred in banking and oil markets.

Other parties, who may impact on the competitive context, are shareholders and channel partners, such as distributors, agents and retailers. As owners, shareholders have viewpoints that may need to be influenced. Channel partners have commercial interests that need to be reconciled. Price structures will be designed to meet their expectations. Prices may take into account the media or pressure groups.

This stage ensures that the potential pricing does not result in adverse reactions from competitors, legislators, customer pressure groups and other bodies.

## Stage 3. Company factors

Fixing the right price begins with a strategic perspective. First, how has price been characterized in the industry? Is there a history of price stability or anarchy? Is the industry vulnerable to price wars? Second, what is your role within the industry? Are you a price leader with a dominant influence over other players in the market? Are you a price follower, responding to the strategy of the Number 1? If there is no price leader, can you see an opportunity to assume the role? Finally, what pricing behaviours could you bring about? The questions establish a realistic context for your own pricing objectives.

## Pricing objectives

Before you can set prices, it is necessary to determine your pricing objectives.

- How do you wish to place or position the company relative to competitors in the eyes of your customers – luxury leader or cheap and cheerful, exclusive or everyday brand?
- Is your objective to grow market share rapidly, or to maximize the value available from existing customers?
- What is your vision for your product, its positioning and pricing over the life-cycle?

The pricing objectives will lead to your plans for pricing over the life-cycle.

## Life-cycle pricing

Convention offers 'competitive pricing' as a strategy where prices are pegged to comparable offers from rivals. This is a reactive approach to pricing. It is not differentiating and may not maximize value capture. See Figure 9.1 for three alternative life-cycle pricing strategies:

1 High remaining high. This is the premium product strategy where the launch price conveys aspiration, luxury or high quality and the continuing price strategy maintains the premium level. An example would be the lager, Stella Artois, brewed by Interbrew (part of Inbev) and now sold in 80 countries. Interbrew has launched the brand in markets outside its home country of Belgium. In each of these markets, Stella Artois has a premium position. For example, in the UK the position is underscored by the tag line, 'Reassuringly expensive'. Premium pricing strategies work effectively when demand is relatively inelastic.

2 High reducing over time. This is the skimming price strategy, often employed with innovative new products. A relatively high launch price meets expectations of selective customers eager to have a new product or service ahead of others and willing to pay a premium for

this novelty. As demand from these early adopters is fulfilled, the company lowers the price progressively, encouraging more mainstream customers to buy the product and thereby widening demand. This strategy delivers a return on development/launch costs and also sets the reference price high enough to make subsequent prices appear particularly good value. An example is the Gillette razor company who have successively introduced innovative shaving systems at relatively high launch prices. These prices have normalized during the product life-cycle. The Trac II twin-blade shaving system was introduced in 1971, the Sensor twin-blade razor system appeared in 1990, succeeded by the SensorExcel a few years later. The Mach3, with three blades, was launched in 1998 achieving high-volume sales, while the technologically more advanced Mach3turbo sells alongside it, at a premium price. Intel have a similar pricing strategy with new processors. Skimming price strategies work effectively when initial demand is relatively inelastic, and mass demand is more elastic.

3  Low remaining low. This is the penetration pricing strategy. A low initial price is set to encourage a very speedy build-up of demand. This price may even be below initial cost of production when there is an expectation that higher volumes will allow a firm to progress rapidly down the experience curve and quickly lower production costs to achieve medium-term profitability. This can act as a barrier to a prospective following brand. Competitors have little time to react as the brand establishes itself in the minds of customers. The on-line retailer, Amazon, is an example of successful penetration pricing. Penetration strategies are popular with intermediaries and channel partners who are attracted by the certainty of high stock-turnover. Penetration strategies succeed when demand is elastic. The risk is that demand elasticity may be over-estimated and volumes may not be achieved in practice.

It is not a viable option to price low initially and then hope to raise prices subsequently. Prices are remarkably inflexible upwards. Customers quickly gain an impression of the benchmark or 'fair' price. They resist any attempt to move brands up-market by raising price

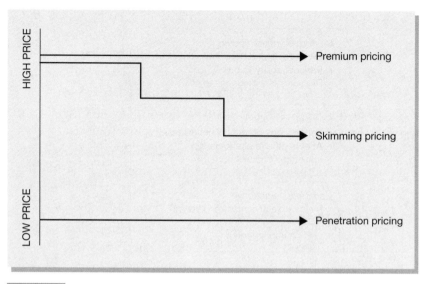

**Figure 9.1** Life-cycle pricing

levels. Unless there is a well-founded and deliberate choice of the penetration strategy, it is a self-limiting strategy to under-price at the outset.

Finally, cross-check that the proposed price provides a return to the company. How does the price compare with the cost price? Establishing the buying or manufacturing cost places a floor below which you cannot go in a profitable transaction. Cost price is not the starting point, rather it is the final part of the process, as a check on financial return.

This stage ensures that the selected price is viable. Figure 9.2 summarizes the three-stage price-setting process.

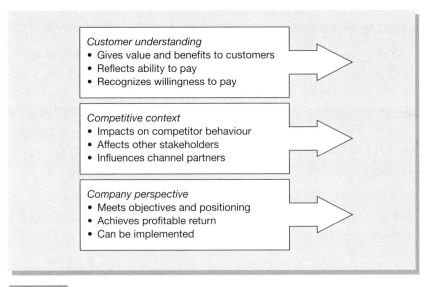

**Figure 9.2**  Setting the price: three-stage process

# Next step: develop a price structure

Price structures are elaborations of fixed prices to address customer price sensitivity and provide incentives to particular behaviours in a matrix that appeals to customers, represents value compared with competition and delivers a profitable return to the vendor. There are two categories:

1  Price scales (second-degree discrimination)

2  Segment criteria (third-degree discrimination).

Quantity discounts are non-linear pricing scales, where a single item is priced at one level and multiple items are charged at discounted levels. Examples are bulk purchase discounts incentivizing customers to buy a greater requirement and store the surplus. For example, rail travellers with First Great Western can buy carnets or sets of ten tickets for the price of nine. The lower price reflects reduced packaging, less administration and staff time for the company. The customer pays a lower unit price but bears the risk that some of the higher quantity may not be used.

A less attractive extension of this approach is the 'Three for the price of two' offer and the 'Buy one, get one free' (BOGOF) promotion. Consumer goods brands find that these offers are attractive to supermarkets to create perceptions of low prevailing prices and encourage impulse purchasing. Nevertheless, deals like these frequently damage the profitability of branded manufacturers since they create spikes in demand with consequent overtime to build stock and downtime after the promotion has taken place. They also sensitize customers to price and encourage shopping by the deal rather than by the benefits.

A smarter way may be to offer a substantial discount when a threshold is reached. HMV, the leading UK retailer of music and DVDs, targeted customers with a promotion offering £5 off when purchases exceeded £35.

Non-linear prices can create opportunities to increase profits. A close understanding of the way in which costs change with quantity can be compared with the customer perceptions of value at different quantity levels. These lines can be graphed to determine widest margins and consequent marketing strategies. For example, when there is high price sensitivity for bulk purchase, the opportunity is to communicate the value of convenience and encourage buying small lots. Conversely the high price of a single unit can be used as a persuasive reference price for quantity purchases.

**Action:** Look at your quantity discount scale. Is it driven by cost variation or by value to buyers? What discount thresholds are conventional in the industry and can you depart from these to gain advantage? Construct scale discounts according to the value received by bulk purchasers, medium-level buyers and small-lot purchasers.

Multi-person pricing is another form of quantity discount. Family tickets for museums and school class packages for Theme Parks encourage group visits that become lucrative with the additional purchases of soft drinks, food and souvenirs. Dolan and Simon (1996) quote the example of an airline aware that spouses may accompany the business traveller. If the price ceiling for the primary traveller is $1,000 and for the spouse is $600, then the airline has a three-way choice:

Charge $1,000 per seat and sell only a single seat – total revenue $1,000.

Charge $600 per seat and sell two seats – total revenue $1,200.

Charge $1,000 for the first seat and $600 for the second seat – total revenue $1,600.

The multi-person discount achieves the highest contribution. Legend has it that a US airline ran such a promotion in the 1970s and subsequently wrote to the wives of the travelling business executives asking how they enjoyed the trip, blind to the incentives they had given to marital infidelity!

**Action:** Analyze the price sensitivity of multiple purchases. What are the triggers to encourage multiple buying?

A reverse form of multi-person discount in the travel industry is the single-person supplement. Given the 'framing effect' previously mentioned, this is unsurprisingly a very unpopular charge, much resented by single travellers. Prices are always more flexible downwards than upwards.

**Action:** Frame price structures to reward extra buying. Avoid structures that appear to penalize the small-scale buyer.

# Reward high users with multi-dimensional prices

Multi-dimensional pricing offers two or more variables so that the price paid can reflect and reward the dynamics of the market place. For example, a daily mileage limit for rental cars surcharges drivers who impose greater wear and tear on vehicles. For example, a Family Rail Card is an up-front payment that gives 33 percent discount off rail tickets bought during the 12-month validity period. This rewards the frequent traveller. Higher commitment in return for lower prices helps the rail company to capture more value.

**Action:** Seek more variables on the price scale. Encourage customers to buy 'season tickets' that give access to lower prices. Find ways of differentiating prices between high maintenance buyers, who require expensive support, and more independent low maintenance buyers.

The multi-dimensional approach allows the vendor choices in ways to increase prices. For example, a company selling industrial gases could impose higher charges on gas across all customers or elect to increase cylinder leasing costs so that faster users (who are more price-sensitive) bear less of the increase and slower users bear more.

# It'll cost you more later

Time-based discounts are also widely used and can be used to capture more value from less price-sensitive customers. Some restaurants have two editions of menus: same dishes, different prices. The determined diners who want to eat after 7.30p.m. will pay more. The more cost-conscious can be persuaded with lower prices to eat out at a less convenient time. This utilizes the facilities of the restaurant and fills the seat for more of the day. Bars offer 'Happy Hours' when fewer people want to drink. Airlines offer lower prices to encourage buying early, travel agents like Lastminute.com offer discounts to clear unsold tickets. Short notice and urgent orders often command a surcharge in business-to-business markets.

**Action:** Consider how to factor time into pricing with a peak-time premium, off-peak special offers, low-priced advanced orders, urgency surcharges and so on.

Time-based discounts can be used creatively. A village in the tourist area of the English Lake District found that a car park extension was needed to cope with car-borne visitors stopping by for a few minutes to photo-graph the renowned view over the lake. To avoid burdening the loyal local shoppers with the bulk of the building costs, they devised an inverse pricing scale. The car park operated with an exit barrier where payment was made. The longer you stayed in the car park the *less* you paid. Hence the visitors paid more, reflecting the full value for a photo-stop. The regular local shoppers stayed longer in the car park and consequently paid less – reflecting the lower value per visit of the car park to them.

**Action:** Think laterally about price structures – maybe you can turn convention on its head.

## Different segment, different price

Segment criteria are the second part of the price structure. Different types of customers may value a product more than others and be persuaded to pay more to obtain this value. Subject to customer perceptions of fairness, prices can be designated for certain segments. Examples are lower-priced admission to cinemas for children and discounted travel for senior citizens. It is necessary to be able to police these segments so that customers in one segment are not able to buy and resell to customers in a higher-priced segment. Wines and spirits brands are faced with this form of arbitrage. Prices vary between geographical markets and there is an incentive for drinkers to purchase in lower-priced markets – Norwegians buy their whisky in lower-priced Sweden, Swedes travel to Denmark for cheaper whisky and the Danes slip over the border into Germany for a bargain bottle. As a consequence, segment criteria in price structures are more often used in services than product sales.

**Action:** Are there segments who value the product or service more highly and, if so, is it practical and acceptable to charge them more? Can the segment criteria be policed to prevent arbitrage?

To sell the same or similar products to different segments at different prices, it is usually necessary to use alternative channels and/or brand names. Black & Decker sell power tools in consumer markets under the Black & Decker brand name. The parent company sells similar tools under the DeWalt brand name via trade channels to industrial users. Each brand has its own price structure, product range, distribution channel and promotional strategy.

## Leading customers up price stairways

In price-sensitive markets with a high elasticity, entry prices are crucial in the battle to gain the attention of customers. If the advertised price is not competitive, then the customer rejects this brand and moves to consider other brands. Smarter pricing means headlining a competitive entry price. Once you have the customers' consideration, you can provide a menu of extras and upgrades that allow them to match their needs for additional services. You create value for different customer types and you are also able to capture the latent value in the market place in the form of higher returns.

An American retailer tested targeted customers with $10 discount voucher when they spent $80 in a single transaction. Few customers responded, but those who took up the offer signalled an opportunity. Their purchases exceeded the threshold set. So the retailer devised a new pricing test – the offer was improved to $10 when customers spent $70. The new trigger level was perceived as much more attractive, being around a 15 percent discount. A large number of customers responded and their average purchases were $106. The attractive offer brought customers into the store. The range and presentation and service from staff moved customers up the volume scale.

Norwich Union, part of Aviva, is a leading player in the ultra-competitive UK car insurance market. They attract drivers with the message 'Let us quote you happy', supported by a survey showing that 58 percent of their customers saved money, 14 percent of them saving over £200. With this promise, customers begin consideration of Norwich Unions' offer. Then the potential upgrades are offered. For a small addition, customers gain access to a 'legal issues' help-line and legal cost cover. Would they also wish to add personal accident cover for loss of sight or loss of limb? European cover? Extra breakdown protection while abroad? Perhaps a courtesy car to be made available while a crashed car is with a repairer. Or even a higher specification model for a slightly higher premium? And with 80 percent of personal injury claims involving soft tissue or whiplash injuries, why not add the 'Physio fast' option? Just £12 per year provides a consultation and up to eight treatment sessions.

**Action:** Headline the offer and usher the customer up the stairway of upgrades.

Competitors may tempt your customers with price structures that promise apparently amazing headline deals. The Morgan Stanley 'buy and fly' Mastercard promises a point with every £10 spent, compared with £20 per point for rival Air Miles. Furthermore, with Morgan Stanley, a spend of only £3,900 is needed to earn a return London to Paris flight (compared with up to £20,000 needed among rivals). Better on two dimensions, yet other credit cards offering free flights should note that Morgan Stanley points expire after only 24 months. This presents an opportunity (and a need) to communicate to customers the value of a longer validity period.

**Action:** Ensure your customers understand the small print conditions when competitors promise lower prices.

In the face of strong competition for travel across the English Channel, P&O Ferries charges a range of prices for different options. There is a peak price for a midday return crossing. The price can be reduced with a semi-flexible ticket that has limited options for subsequent changes. Alongside this tariff, P&O offers promotional fares for a single crossing, tied to particular off-peak times. The promotional price is structured on the assumption that these customers will generate additional income and benefits (as shown in Table 9.1). For one thing, the fare acts as an advertisement for and an opportunity to sample the product, as the cost is low enough for some customers to treat it as an impulse purchase. Second, if travellers miss the specified crossing times, the price rises. There are upgrade options giving priority when loading and disembarking. And P&O factors in further profit opportunities on board, where travellers are likely to buy meals, beers, wines, spirits or souvenirs.

**Table 9.1**    Price structures for profit, cross-channel ferry example

|  | Customer | Company |
|---|---|---|
| Pay more get more | Upgrade for priority loading<br>Peak-time crossing<br>Flexible ticket | Revenue benefit (direct) |
| Pay less get less | Off-peak crossing<br>Restricted time away<br>Semi-flexible ticket<br>Penalty for later crossing | Potential revenue benefit (indirect), e.g. sales of food, souvenirs, wine |

Financial services markets are particularly competitive because interest rates are readily comparable. Hence HSBC Bank credit cards offered an appealing introductory rate, 0 percent on purchases for six months, in mid-2005, but build profitability through the foibles of account holders by charging £20 for late payments and £20 for exceeding credit limits.

**Action:** Consider penalties for missing discount conditions and rewards for buying upgrades.

# Block out competitors – pair up product and system

Competitors may sometimes be held at bay through separating two elements of a package. This is a tied consumables model. A subsidized master product, say an electric toothbrush, is offered that requires a consumable part, say a brushing head. The master product is patent protected such that other manufacturers are precluded from producing consumables that fit this system. By designing a printer as a machine with a proprietary ink cartridge, Hewlett Packard (HP) are able to succeed in a highly competitive market. HP win customers with a superior design of printer. It is sold at a competitive price to establish the HP system among customers and then capture value through the sale of HP ink cartridges. Similarly, telephone handsets are provided at low or no cost in order to win customers for profitable airtime contracts.

The advantage of this system is that it creates a customer familiarity with the system that builds into a psychological switching cost. To move away from the supplier of the master product a customer must engage with an alternative supplier, replace the old system and learn the characteristics of the new system. As long as the customer perceives that value is provided, loyalty persists. Easy and convenient availability of the consumable is a success criterion to inculcate this loyalty. Any difficulty or shortfall can create openings for vendors of alternative systems. This is a smart way to capture value in the market by excluding competitors after the initial deal is won.

**Action:** Consider how to design a system using the tied consumables model.

# Hot sauce calls for a refreshing bundle

Another form of smart pricing that can capture more value from customers is the price bundle. A bundle is where customers are persuaded to buy a package of goods or services rather than a single item. The South African restaurant chain, Nando's, with restaurants from Karachi to Coventry, offers a bundled soft drink package. You can have as many refills as you need to quench your thirst after eating Nando's chicken spiced with their unique peri-peri sauce. A more sophisticated bundle is offered by Charles Schwab who gives investment advice, products and services in competition with Internet traders. Schwab has bundled in added-value items like better research tools with its investment services in order to command higher commissions.

The car industry has used pricing structures and bundling for many years to raise the value of its sales. See the Mini One. It is advertised at a price, on top of which a choice of three option packs, branded Salt, Pepper or Chilli, tempts buyers to 'spice up' their chosen vehicle. The packs include cosmetic features, as well as features known to be advantageous when reselling cars – seat height adjustment, for example. For some customers, then, the extras become an obligatory part of the purchase.

**Action:** Consider features that are highly valued by customers, such that they could be bundled in with a complete package to command a premium price.

Bundled propositions can also move customers up the revenue ladder. An example is provided by Eurostar, the passenger train company operating between London and Paris, Lille and Brussels. A customer rings the call centre to buy a return trip to Lille for a weekend with his wife. The cost is £115 per person. This price establishes a benchmark in the mind of the customer, who responds with the question, 'Have you a better deal than that?' The agent offers a bundled package including two nights' accommodation and first class travel for £180 per person. The customer calculates that for £65 more he is getting first-class seating that brings with it a three-course meal and complimentary wine (outbound and again on the return to the UK). In addition the £65 includes two nights' accommodation in an approved hotel in old Lille – no hassle or risk in locating and booking a hotel himself.

**Action:** Look for opportunities to combine standard prices with a higher-priced bundle of benefits that represents good value in comparison with the benchmark of the standard price.

Today, some companies are using bundling as a way of keeping the brand at the forefront of the customers' minds. For instance, children will hold on to the Disney toy long after they finish the McDonald's Happy Meal.

**Action:** Identify packages of benefits that include mementoes to stimulate positive memories and items to encourage word-of-mouth recommendation.

## When they bundle, I'll be different

As competitors provide bundles, it may be smart to move in the opposite direction. Publishers are selling downloadable book chapters individually to match business school course requirements. New value is created by breaking up products previously seen as integrated. Most public relations firms charge fees in the form of a monthly retainer. According to George Mannes (2005), writing in *Fast Company*, new agency PayPerClip bases its charges on a rate for each successful press cutting. Payment by results distinguished PayPerClip from rivals and 32 clients signed up between June and December 2004. Some customers may prefer to construct their own tailored offering from a series of priced menu options. The supplying company can pass design costs to the customer, and also gains customer involvement and commitment to the process.

Nagle and Cressman (2002), writing in *Marketing Management*, cite a printing company offering high-level services bundled in with sales of units of printing. The company was faced with lower-priced competitors who did not offer the same added value services. Potential customers would challenge prices with quotations from these rivals. The result: costs were high and profits disappointing. The solution for this company was to identify which of its added value services made a difference to customers and charge for these services separately. Examples were:

- correcting files
- adapting to late delivery of files
- redesigning a job to save mailing costs
- reducing colour variability
- scheduling jobs at peak times.

The result was that customers either paid extra costs willingly or changed their behaviour in ways that eliminated costs for the company. The new pricing structure gave customers a choice: basic service at a lower cost (comparable to rivals) or higher service benefits with a correspondingly higher cost. By unbundling, the company became more price competitive.

**Action:** Uncover opportunities to deconstruct offerings giving customers menu-based options.

## Confused by prices? That's the intention

Where customers are able readily to compare prices, they are expected to choose the lower prices. Brands in price-sensitive markets with low switching costs, like telecommunications, attempt to obstruct these comparisons with confusion pricing. Each brand develops unique complex price structures. Each supplier can make a 'lowest price' claim for one or other package. For example, prices for phone calls will vary by time of day, day of week, call length and caller destination or network. Up to a threshold, calls will be included within the monthly rental payment. Six different parameters mean that the customer would need to understand precisely his or her own future usage mix to calculate which supplier represented best value. One phone user observed that it would take six months to work out the best deal, by which time price scales would have changed half a dozen times!

The benefit of confusion pricing strategies is that customers are bewildered and will select brands on non-price grounds, such as service and other benefits. For this reason, high levels of service satisfaction are essential to build customer loyalty. The disadvantage of confusion pricing is that consumers know they are being confused and their trust in suppliers diminishes. Less trust means less loyalty and a risk of defection to other suppliers who appear to be more transparent.

**Action:** Seek ways to make prices less comparable with competitors in parallel with customer relationship strategies. Be wary of levels of complexity that customers distrust.

# End confusion, risk a price war

In spring 1992, American Airlines interpreted market research showing customer dissatisfaction with confusing flight prices as an opportunity to lead the travel industry into a new era of simplified fares. Chief Executive Bob Crandall launched 'Value pricing' on 29 April 1992. Fares were made easy to understand with only four fare levels: First, Regular coach, Discount coach (seven days in advance) and Discount coach (21 days in advance). Customers responded positively. Competitors were threatened. The book *Power Pricing* by Dolan and Simon tells the story of the competitive response. Major rivals, Delta and United Airlines matched prices immediately. Smaller airlines took their prices lower and on 26 May, North West Airlines reacted strongly with a two for one summer offer to families headlined 'Grown-ups fly free'. Within three months a full-scale price war ensued. Customers had a summer of amazingly cheap fares. Airline share prices dropped by over 20 percent. Major airlines lost money, smaller companies went under. After the summer, it was American Airlines who ended the price war with a return to complex fare structures that customers could not understand.

According to the journal *Airline Business*, European airlines have acted more cautiously in restructuring complex fares in response to no-frills operators. British Airways and Lufthansa began the process in 2002. By 2003, British Airways had overhauled its complex fare structure of 2 million fares into three basic types of ticket. Lufthansa also simplified fare classes and removed restrictions. Revenue management means that cheapest fares are not usually available seven days before departure. Late buyers are less price-sensitive. Transparent price structures are perceived to be fairer.

**Action:** Role-play competitor responses before introducing new price structures lest they force or tempt competitors into price wars.

The euro provides price transparency across much of Europe and it makes inter-country price comparison in industrial markets much easier for international buyers. For suppliers this carries the threat of standardization at the lowest country price. The answer is to impede easy price comparison. Writing in *McKinsey Quarterly*, Ahlberg, Garemo and Naucler (1999) recommend using a cornucopia of approaches: country discount scales, varying terms and conditions from country to country, using pricing models based on loyalty, differentiating product features, packaging and service levels, bundling services with products and introducing service contracts. Standardizing prices at the level of the lowest price anywhere passes value to customers. To capture optimal value in each geographical segments, the answer is to match actual prices paid in each country with willingness and ability to pay.

**Action:** Manage international price structures to minimize cross-country price comparisons and the risk of arbitrage.

## Price structure gets golfers out on the links

Price structures can impact on usage. For example, John Gourville and Dilip Soman (2002) identified that annual membership payments result in club members using facilities heavily initially but declining subsequently. He found that quarterly payments stimulate spikes in demand every three months as members are reminded by their bank statements to get value by using the facilities. Therefore, price structures can be used to stimulate usage, and payment structures can be timed to even out demand across the year or meet other business objectives.

**Action:** Think how price structures can support desirable customer behaviour.

# It's new, what should I charge?

Pricing places a new product in the spectrum very effectively. Cynical customers disregard advertising claims. The volume of other messages distracts attention from a benefit story. The one concrete aspect of a product launch is the price. It demonstrates how the 'experts' in the selling company value the new product compared with existing alternatives. Therefore, the initial price of a new product is a powerful message to the market. It sets a reference price. Managers may be eager to build awareness and demand. Often they will consider a low price to command attention, hoping to lift prices when volume sales are captured. Logical thought but a mistake. Customers will recall the first price they paid and resent any later increase.

Better strategies are to set high release prices to position the product appropriately for the longer term. To meet short-term launch objectives customers – aware of the true price – can be offered samples. In industrial markets, trial periods can be offered. For consumer products, bite-sized packs are often made available at an appropriate fraction of the running price, so that the financial risk for the first-time buyer is smaller and the value is still maintained.

Pricing experts Marn, Roegner and Zawada (2003), writing in *McKinsey Quarterly* recommend that new products are first categorized into three types:

- Revolutionary products that need explaining to the market.
- Evolutionary products that represent upgrades to existing products.
- Me-too products.

Each type requires a different pricing approach for launch. The me-too will normally have a small range of pricing options because it offers little differentiation from what is already priced in the market. The evolutionary product will have a wider scope for pricing – it is important that new products with significantly superior benefits are not under-priced. This may force competitors who are threatened into retaliatory price cuts which destabilize the market. Revolutionary products have the widest scope for pricing decisions. Given the need to explain and communicate the benefits, it is essential that prices are carefully chosen, so that margins are available to fund this. It is better to begin with a price at the top end of the desired range. If sales are slow, the price can always be reduced.

Marn, Roegner and Zawada (2003) warn that companies routinely overlook the higher reaches of their pricing potential for new products. Price structures for new and existing products should aim to claim their true value.

## Chapter takeaways

- Over-pricing is rare and is normally corrected when sales disappoint. Under-pricing occurs significantly more often and damages brands when profits are foregone and products are positioned at a lower level in the market place.

- Setting the smart price is a three stage process that considers:
  - customer factors, such as value received, ability and willingness to pay;
  - competitive factors such as the impact the price will have on rivals and how it may influence their behaviour;
  - company factors such as the actual and desired role in the industry, the target positioning in the market place. Finally, a check to ensure the proposed price provides an adequate financial return.

- Three options exist for pricing over the life-cycle:

  Premium – price high initially and remains high;

  Skimming – price high and progressively reduces;

  Penetration – price low from the start to gain sales rapidly.

  There is no fourth option of pricing low initially with the aim of increasing later.

- Quantity discounts, multi-dimensional terms and time-based structures can increase revenues and profits.

- Where arbitrage is difficult or impossible, for example in services, different prices can be charged to different segments.

- Successful price structures move customers up price stairways. Bundling can achieve the same.

- Confusion pricing is an option in price-sensitive markets with low switching costs but the practice risks losing customer trust.

## Management questions for your business

- Does our price-setting process factor in value to the customer, ability to pay and the influence of reference prices on willingness to pay? Does it consider the impact on competitors and other parties?

- How has price been characterized in the industry? Is there a history of price stability or anarchy? Is the industry vulnerable to price wars?

- What is our pricing role within the industry? Are we the price leader with a dominant influence over other players in the market? Are we a price follower, responding to the strategy of the Number 1? If there is no price leader, is there an opportunity to assume the role?

- Which life-cycle strategy best applies to our business?

- Is our price structure capturing value from different customer groups? Where could we be more creative?

- How could we lead customers up price stairways, block competitors out and diminish customers' ability to compare our prices?

## Going further – references and additional reading

Ahlberg, J., Garemo, N., and Naucler, T. (1999) 'The euro: how to keep your prices up and your competitors down' *McKinsey Quarterly*, 2.

*Airline Business* (2005) 'A simpler life – Delta Airlines and KLM set to overhaul pricing structure', 1 February.

*Daily Telegraph* (2005) 'When choosing your car's colour, consider the impact on its value when you sell', 28 May.

Dolan, R. J. and Simon, H. (1996) *Power Pricing*, The Free Press, New York, NY.

Gourville, J. and Soman, D. (2002) 'Pricing and the psychology of consumption', *Harvard Business Review*, September.

Lester, T. (2002) 'How to ensure the price is exactly right', *Financial Times*, 30 January.

Mannes, G. (2005) 'The urge to unbundle', *Fast Company*, February.

Marn, M., Roegner, E. and Zawada, C. C. (2003) 'Pricing new products', *McKinsey Quarterly*, 3.

McNealy, S. (2001) 'Welcome to the bazaar', *Harvard Business Review*, March.

Nagle, T. T. and Cressman, C. E. (2002) 'Don't just set prices, manage them', *Marketing Management*, November.

Simon, H. and Dolan, R. J. (1998) 'Price customisation', *Marketing Management*, Fall.

Warwick-Ching, L. (2005) 'Borrowers urged to reach for the sky', *Financial Times*, 23 April.

Watson, S. (2003) 'The long and the short of pricing', *Directions – Ashridge Journal*, Summer.

www.simon-kucher.com

# 10

# Communicating prices – creating positive perceptions

Price communications are normally deal-focused. New low prices are broadcast. Starbursts in advertisements promise higher discounts and price is highlighted as the reason to buy. *Marketing Magazine* provides a monthly analysis of UK consumer recall of advertisements, known as Presswatch. This chart is often topped by a price-led advertiser. An example comes from the white goods retailer Currys, which is rarely out of the top five. Press adverts by Currys have a consistent formula: busy with numerous small illustrations of products overlaid with prices and savings, offers of extended credit and time-limited exclusive offers.

This simple strategy suits price-led discounters. But it puts pressure on competitors who have a complex story of benefits to convey. How should they answer the question posed by discounters: 'Why pay more?'

Before we answer this question, let us look at how price communication works in practice.

## Pricing cues – the magic of 99p

There are a number of pricing cues that buyers understand. The most obvious is the word 'sale' alongside products in retail outlets. Research by Anderson and Simester (2003) shows that displaying 'sale' beside the price of an item in a mail order catalogue (with or without actually varying the price) can increase demand by more then 50 percent. Of course, retailers can (and some do) mislead consumers with non-genuine sale offers. Misuse of this tactic is controlled by legislation, media attention and the limits of consumer credibility. A small number of 'sale' signs will increase customer purchases. Too many 'sale' signs will diminish overall sales.

Another common pricing cue is using a 9 at the end of a price to signify a bargain. Academic research in the 1950s and the 1960s identified the popularity of prices ending in 9s. Does the digit 0 tend to create a prestige effect that deters price-conscious shoppers? In research published in 2000, M. A. Stiving proposed an economic model where firms wishing to convey quality with high prices should use the digit 0 as the rightmost digit and those operating in low-quality segments should use the digit 9 for their price endings.

Sandra Naipaul and H. G. Parsa (2001) applied this hypothesis to dining out, studying prices on 231 restaurant menus. Of 3,290 menu items from the 62 high-end restaurants only 13 percent ended with the digit 9. Looking at low-end restaurants, 63 percent of menu items ended in the digit 9. Incidentally, the research had to treat Chinese restaurants separately because according to ancient Chinese traditions and beliefs the digits 6 and 8 are the most preferred for price endings, the digit 4 is considered inauspicious and the use of the digit 9 is not allowed as it is reserved for the Emperor.

The conclusions of Naipaul and Parsa (2001) supported signalling theory. This states that sellers know the quality of their goods and services prior to the sale and prospective buyers are less well informed. Therefore sellers convey quality through signals that are interpreted and used by the buyers in making decisions.

Research by Anderson and Simester (2003) shows signalling to be remarkably effective in retail pricing. Specifically, in a women's clothing catalogue, sales rose by a third when a dress originally priced at $34 was increased to $39. A further test with the price raised to $44 showed the same demand as at $34. In another experiment, customers of a catalogue clothing firm were randomly mailed with one of two price versions and the sales results were analyzed by Professor Robert Schindler working with Thomas Kibarian. The version with prices ending in 99 cents outperformed the version with round number pricing by 8 percent.

Prices ending in 9 signify that you should buy for a price reason. Round-number pricing conveys that you are buying for a broader spectrum of qualitative reasons. Dentists charge round numbers for their treatments. Ecco shoes price their entry level shoes at £64.99 to convey a bargain, whereas their standard and premium footwear are priced in round numbers such as £85.00, to convey that price is a less important factor in the choice process.

Pricing cues are most effective where customers' knowledge of prices is poor. They are most effective on items that are purchased infrequently, where prices vary seasonally or for items targeted at new buyers.

# Err . . . I don't know how much it is normally

In fact, customers' knowledge of retail prices is generally poor. With the typical household buying several hundred different items from the supermarket each week, most customers do not know individual product prices and would be reluctant even to guess. Prices vary considerably week-to-week, store-to-store and items are no longer price-marked as barcodes and shelf markers replace individual price tags in leading supermarkets.

Instead of knowing each price, customers use prices of key items as benchmarks. These are called known value indicators. In the UK a standard loaf of white sliced bread, a kilogram pack of white sugar and 415gm tin of Heinz baked beans are known value indicators. Customers infer prices from such 'signposts' to judge where an outlet falls in the price spectrum. Popular items bought more frequently signal the value of more expensive items – the price of tennis balls is a proxy for the competitiveness of tennis racquet pricing. A plain white T-shirt could indicate the price position of a clothing store. Anderson and Simester (2003) recommend that sellers identify and signpost products that are popular, where customers are likely to hold an accurate idea of the benchmark price and which are complementary to the more expensive items.

Two further signalling devices are used by retailers to influence the perceptions of shoppers. These are bracketing manoeuvres, one high and the other low. To ensure that customers notice low price levels, one or two 'breathtaking bargains' will hit them early in their first steps into the store – IKEA use this technique in stores from the Netherlands to Canada. Tesco promotes petrol and car insurance in posters on their many delivery vehicles because, for many segments, these are highly price-sensitive products.

The other signalling device is the high-end contrast. Thomas Nagle highlights the importance of setting reference prices. The aim is to place a reference price in the mind of the buyer, against which the product the customer eventually chooses will appear good value. This applies in industrial and consumer markets. Sometimes called 'top-down' selling, the salesperson initially presents a product above the buyer's price range. As the discussion progresses, the seller presents lower priced items to suit the buyer's budget and these appear good value by comparison with the initial reference point. The test vehicle at a motor dealership will be top of its range, so that the model actually selected will seem good value in comparison.

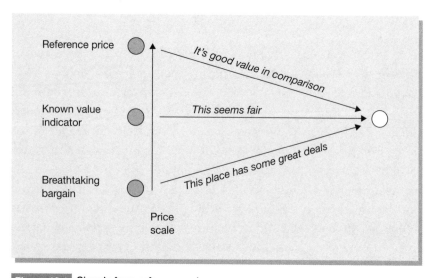

**Figure 10.1** Signals from reference prices

# Seeing something else pricey loosens the wallet

Going further, two academics, Joseph Nunes and Peter Boatwright (2004) believe that non-related or incidental prices can act as reference points that shape perceptions and willingness to pay. Their studies demonstrate that unrelated prices encountered during the purchase process can effect what people will pay. Believe it or not, if customers see an unrelated high price just before the transaction they are willing to pay more!

The proof? They analyzed six years of sales data from one of the best-known car auctioneers in the USA, selecting classic car auctions where buyers are normally equipped with historical prices and the industry 'blue guide' to prices. Between 1995 and 2000, 1,477 classic automobiles were auctioned. Their findings conclusively proved that the price premium secured by the preceding lot will affect the price achieved on the succeeding car. When the bid on the first car exceeded the blue book value by more than 100 percent, there was a carry-over effect and the average price of the second car was 39 percent over book. The higher the premium on car one, the greater the echo on car two.

More proof? The researchers compared the effect on prices paid for CDs when they were sold near to sweatshirts at two different price levels. When the sweatshirts retailed at $80, people paid an average of $9.00 for the CD. When the sweatshirts were priced at $10, the average price paid was $7.29. Same day, same location, same CD. The only factor to change was the price marking on the nearby sweatshirt stand. None of the shoppers interviewed afterwards believed that the price of the unrelated product had affected their judgement. Clearly it had occurred sublimi-nally.

The lesson is that consumers' willingness to pay can vary systematically with the price of unrelated products present in the shopping environment. This might influence retailers to place expensive goods in the shopping environment. Catalogue retailers might include luxury items in the early pages. Industrial products might be sold in conjunction with recommendations for unrelated but more expensive goods.

The final price cue is the 'price guarantee'. This is a promise to match or even beat any competitor. This provides reassurance to the buyer that, should they find a cheaper price elsewhere in the period after the purchase, then the difference will be refunded. The department store, John Lewis uses this approach (see Chapter 6) as part of their brand positioning. Some retailers in ultra-competitive markets extend promises to commit to refund 'double the difference' to add further drama to the guarantee. Price matching promises are reassuring to customers who feel able to progress to a purchase without comparison shopping.

Research into price-matching policies by University of Houston's Professor James Hess and University of California at Davis' Professor Eitan Gerstner found two results of price-matching policies:

- Price-matching policies reduce the amount of price dispersion in the market – meaning that customers will find the same price in each store.

- Price-matching policies tend to result in higher prices – the policies are directed equally at competitors to convey that if you drop your price, we will bring ours down too. This can diminish price competition in markets.

In selling to a major customer, it can be effective to guarantee that no other customer will receive a better price.

In business-to-business markets, price-matching policies can be seen as anti-competitive. Anderson and Simester (2003) warn that such policies may breach competition law. Guidance on anti-trust implications is given in Appendix 2 of *The Price Advantage* by Marn, Roegner and Zawada (2004).

## Threshold price points

Price setters must take into account psychological thresholds of pricing points above which demand is forecast to fall off considerably. The UK white goods industry holds that there is a £199 psychological barrier for refrigerators and washing machines (see Figure 10.2). If entry prices exceed this threshold, it is believed that customers will be discouraged. A European Union Directive will require manufacturers to manage the cost of taking away and recycling consumers' old products. According to Claire Murphy (2005) writing in *Marketing Magazine*, manufacturers want this presented as '£199 plus £5 recycling levy'. On the other hand, the UK government fears that the cost will be perceived by consumers as another tax and want the levy included in the list price. Laws in South Africa require advertised prices to include all taxes and surcharges.

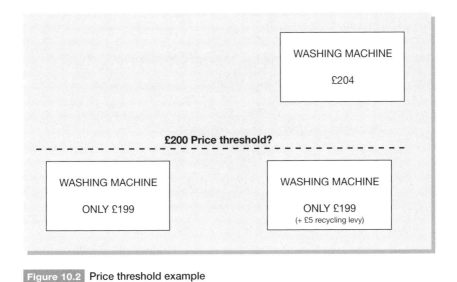

WASHING MACHINE

£204

**£200 Price threshold?**

WASHING MACHINE

ONLY £199

WASHING MACHINE

ONLY £199
(+ £5 recycling levy)

**Figure 10.2** Price threshold example

There are dangers to brands if they try to hold on to a price threshold and cheapen the product in the face of inflation. In the 1960s, cocoa prices rose on the world market. Year by year, Cadburys reduced the size and thickness of their Cadbury Dairy Milk chocolate bar rather than exceed the one shilling threshold. Gradually the bars got less and less appealing to customers. Rival, Rowntree, became aware of the opportunity and launched the thicker and more expensive Yorkie bar with great success.

Some price thresholds are valid. Often price thresholds are specific to a region or a particular competitive set of retailers. Some are industry myths. Many were swept away in Europe by the introduction of the euro, when manufacturers had to determine pricing scales in the new currency.

**Action:** Challenge and validate psychological price thresholds.

# Price presentation

There are many ways to present prices. Usability expert, Kristoffer Bohmann, counts ten variations in communicating prices to retail consumers ranging from the basic '*$10*', through '*Price $10 (45 percent off)*' to the complex '*Retail price $18.00. Our price $10.00*'.

Consider the following thoughts on price presentation:

| Presentation | Desired customer perception |
|---|---|
| €20 | Simply a functional communication of a regular price |
| €19.99 | Here is a deal or a bargain |
| Sale: only €20 | I can get this at sale price |
| Price €20: you save €5 | I can save money here |
| Was €25, now €20 | The price has come down |
| €20 (25 percent off) | This is a big discount |
| Our price €20 | This price is lower than competitors |
| €20: rebate €5 | I had better buy today before the rebate ends |
| Handwritten tag | They've just cut the price |
| Printed price tag | This is a regular price |
| Prices include VAT | This is all inclusive |
| Prices exclude VAT | I have to pay tax on top of this! |
| Prices exclude delivery | This is a showroom price and there are add-ons |

This list is not exhaustive. It demonstrates that there are many ways of presenting prices to convey the price and the desired context to influence the customers' perceptions.

**Action:** Document the specific impression you wish to create with price lists and consider how best could you achieve this.

## The Machiavellian way to communicate

Prices are often persuasively presented in terms of a bundle. The value of the bundle price can be supported by a series of figures showing the effective discount off each element within the bundle. The framing effect (see Chapter 4) tells us that customers respond positively to news of gains – so give them many gains. On the other hand, if the bundle price has to go up, quote only the single total increase – minimize the news of 'losses'. Follow Machiavelli's advice:

*Severities should be dealt out all at once, so that their suddenness may give less offence.*

*Benefits ought to be handed out drop by drop, so that they may be relished the more.*

*Niccolo Machiavelli*

In writing about the framing effect in *Critical Eye*, Professor John Walsh (2005) quotes Machiavalli advising rulers to use this tactic of maximizing good news and minimizing bad news.

## Divide and conquer

Price may be presented as a single annual amount, or a monthly or daily sum. Irrationally, presenting the daily sum can create a lower price perception.

**Table 10.1**  Presenting prices: annual, monthly or daily?

| | |
|---|---|
| Price $360 per year | Index 100 |
| Price $30 per month | Index 300 |
| Price $1 per day | Index 1,000 |

Marn, Roegner and Zawada (2004) give an instance where a term insurance provider offered options like those above. Quoting monthly amounts resulted in three times higher take-up and daily sums were ten times more popular. This held true even when the actual payments were made every 180 days for all the options.

**Action:** Consider the duration of the experience and check ways to represent the total price as a daily rate or a fractional amount.

# Here is the price . . . plus one last benefit

Sales trainers teach a way to overcome the negative effects of communicating price in a sales transaction. The technique is to present the product benefits, give the price and then add one additional benefit, so that the final customer impression is that he or she is receiving value. Altered Image, a hairdresser in Berkhamsted, England, adds to the foot of their receipt the phrase 'Hope we have made the difference. We look forward to seeing you on _____ (date of next appointment).' The added value is a diary reminder.

**Action:** Seek out small additional benefits that could be communicated after the price is advised in order to leave the final positive impression.

# Love discounts, hate surcharges

When prices are presented in price lists, adjustments to the price scale will be included, perhaps discounts for quantity or surcharges for urgent deliveries. These are also a key part of price communication. Losses or surcharges are weighed much more heavily than gains or discounts – the framing effect. Surcharges will therefore attract proportionately more negative attention than the positive effect of discounts. So the conventional advice is to present top-end prices and then allow discounts off these amounts, rather than presenting low-end prices and adding surcharges.

There is an exception to this rule. If the surcharge you add directs blame to another party, it can underline your commitment to good value. EasyJet advertise low come-on prices, such as flights for £4.99. As the booking is made, taxes are added to these low prices (blame the government), charges are added (blame the airports) and credit card fees are added (blame the banks). Lufthansa adds a kerosene surcharge to send the blame to the oil companies.

**Action:** Focus positive attention with your discount scale, unless there is an appropriate opportunity to add a surcharge ascribed to another party, which places you in a good light by implication.

## Why should I clear my own table?

Price communication goes beyond simply presenting the price. Companies must also use other ways to draw attention to the benefits of their price strategy. The furniture retailer, IKEA focuses attention on low prices and finds numerous ways to remind customers of this price stance. For instance, a notice at IKEA, in Brent Park, London, states:

*At IKEA, clearing your own table at the end of your meal is one of the reasons you paid less at the start! By taking your tray to a tray station we can continue to keep our prices low. It also means our staff have more time to serve you and to cook.*

*It's a piece of cake!*

Even in their restaurant they find a way to remind customers of the low prices they are receiving!

Premium brands operate at the other end of the spectrum and support their prices by communicating how everything is included in a comprehensive service operation – it is all done for you.

## What a rising price says about you

The price today compared with the price last week can also convey a message. We saw earlier that where the price trend is downward, it is necessary to give customers a reason to buy today rather than delay the purchase. Price deflation in Japan has made life difficult for many industries where purchasers simply hold back for the next price drop. By contrast, an upward price trend is a positive encouragement to customers to buy now. Industrial tenders with short validity periods may encourage buyers to commit lest the price goes up. If raw material prices are rising, this can be a wise approach to capture value from customers. Allowing a long validity period encourages customers to delay and may mean prices charged do not reflect the reduced margin of interim cost rises. Explaining that the price cannot be guaranteed for longer than, say, one month, presses the buyer to come to a decision.

The building industry endeavours to manage prices of home developments, so that the first properties are sold relatively inexpensively and then subsequent properties are released at progressively higher prices. The message is clear. Buy today, for these properties are in demand and they will be more expensive if you delay. The value message will be eagerly supported by early buyers in their word-of-mouth recommendations. Writing in *Professional Builder*, Bill Lurz (2002), quotes Don Tomnitz, CEO of US housebuilders DR Horton.

*It is important that prices climb steadily. We want our buyers to see that they're achieving a substantial rate of appreciation in their homes. If you raise prices steadily, as you sell through each tenth of the project, by the end you've got nine-tenths of your buyers feeling really good and the last tenth glad they squeaked in.*

The best example of price management over a number of years is the appreciating price of diamonds. Historically, by releasing restricted quantities of diamonds on to the market and by communicating the way prices have appreciated, the industry has built a long-term image of value at the high end of the price range. 'A diamond is forever.'

## Chapter takeaways

- There are a number of price cues that guide buyers: the value message of a price ending in 9, the quality message of round number pricing, signalling devices like known value indicators and price guarantees.

- Reference prices are important to set the context – related items and even incidental products with higher prices can support your pricing.

- Price presentation – different ways of expressing prices can create different customer perceptions.
- Customers love discounts and hate surcharges – there are smart ways to use this in communications.
- Managing a rising price can build customer confidence.

## Management questions for your business

- What signalling devices do we use currently?
- Which of our products need value pricing with a 9 ending and where should we use round numbers?
- How well do we manage perceptions with reference prices?
- What would be the effect of price guarantees on us, our customers and our competitors?
- What are the threshold prices in our product ranges? Have we validated them?
- What impression does our price list create? What impression would we like it to give?
- Could we use surcharges to shift blame on to third parties?

## Going further – references and additional reading

Anderson, E. and Simester, D. (2003) 'Mind your pricing cues', *Harvard Business Review*, November.

Hess, J. and Gerstner, E. (1991) 'Price matching policy: an empirical case', *Managerial and Decision Economics*, Summer.

Lurz, B. (2002) 'Pricing opens the door to profit', *Professional Builder*, May.

*Marketing Magazine Presswatch* – a monthly survey conducted by Taylor Nelson Sofres.

Marn, M. V., Roegner, E. V. and Zawada, C. C. (2004) *The Price Advantage*, Wiley, Hoboken, NJ – see Appendix 2 'Anti-trust issues'.

Murphy, C. (2005) 'Rising costs please pass it on', *Marketing Magazine*, 31 March.

Naipaul, S. and Parsa, H. G. (2001) 'Menu price endings that communicate value and quality', *Cornell Hotel and Restaurant Administration Quarterly*, February.

Nunes, J. C. and Boatwright, P. (2001) 'Pricey encounters', *Harvard Business Review*, July and (2004) 'Incidental prices and their effect on willingness to pay', *Journal of Marketing Research*, November.

Stiving, M. A. (2000) 'Price ending: when price signals quality', *Journal of Management Science*, 46 (12) December.

Walsh, J. (2005) 'Grasping the psychology of pricing pays', *Critical Eye*, June.

www.bohmann.dk – usability expert Kristoffer Bohmann.

# 11

# Why pay more? How to get higher prices

Now let us consider the challenging question, posed by competitors offering lower prices, 'Why pay more?' Customers need a reason and smarter pricing can provide it.

There are nine communication tactics to convey superior benefits – some tangible, some emotional. All are designed to increase customers' willingness to pay.

### 1 Genuinely better product, clearly communicated

Customers will pay more for quality when the product superiority is made visible and evident. Openness matters and dramatic communications can draw attention to the better product.

Heinz changed the recipe of its cream of tomato soup in 2004. Originally launched in 1910, it was selling at a rate of 500,000 tins per week. Every day Heinz used enough tomatoes making it to fill an Olympic-sized swimming pool. But poor margins compared with chilled soups and health trends against salt levels and criticism from the Food Standards Agency led Heinz to create a new recipe with 20 percent less salt, 18 percent less fat and 13 percent more tomatoes. In addition to revising their existing recipes, Heinz introduced nine new varieties of soup including 'carrot with ginger' and 'sweet potato and rosemary'. They worked with cookbook writer and former project manager at the Good Housekeeping Research Institute, Liz Trigg. Heinz developed flavours that tasted less processed and closer to homemade ones. Production tasks were changed and over £250,000 worth of new machinery was installed.

The new soup range was launched in August 2004. Trigg said that 'every ingredient can be found in most cupboards or bought at your local supermarket'. In fact, true to her word, Heinz invited the food writer of ivillage.co.uk and the food correspondents of other media to a cook-off. They were provided with recipes such as 'spicy butternut squash', donned aprons, chopped and stirred and cooked soup from scratch. The journalists were then invited to compare their own results with the Heinz tinned variants. Jennifer Howze of ivillage gave the verdict: 'Both versions were yummy with a nice taste of squash with just a bit of zing from chilli.'

To bring about the change, Heinz recruited about 20,000 'souper troopers' with 1,000 lorries to clear around 6 million tins of the old soups from supermarket shelves in one day and replace them with the new recipe cans. All the soup removed from the shelves was donated to the Salvation Army – an international Christian charity combining spiritual and social ministry.

What were the results of the new recipes and the publicity around them?

Heinz increased prices by 20 percent with cream of tomato soup rising from around 49p per can to 59p for the new recipe. The company negotiated a 25–30 percent increase in its share of space for soup in big supermarkets. Heinz saw its brand category value rise by more than £1.4 million in the final quarter of 2004 and the 'Special' range gained 6 percent household penetration within 16 weeks of launch.

## 2  Highlight the risks

A major reason for customers to pay more is to obtain security and avoid risks. Contemporary economists are aware that human economic behaviour is not as rational as theoretical economists once believed. Where the outcomes of a series of exchanges are predictable as an overall average but unpredictable for any specific transaction, most people prefer to avoid the risk of making a loss, rather than take the chance of making a gain. This is true, even when the average expected outcome of the two actions would be the same. The motivation to avoid losses is greater than the appeal of the gains. *The Economist* magazine speculated that this may be a consequence of evolution. In nature, with a food supply that is often barely adequate, losses that lead to the pangs of hunger are felt more keenly than the gains that lead to the comfort of being sated. For whatever reason, customers will likely pay more to avoid risks of losses.

As a house price bubble nears its peak, potential buyers are wary of taking on commitments lest house prices fall and they come to own a property with negative equity. In other words, their houses can only be sold for less than the value of the mortgage. Newcastle Building Society and mortgage broker John Charcol devised a creative solution. Within the package, mortgage payment protection covers monthly payments for up to a year if the borrower is unable to work following redundancy, accident or sickness. If during this time, the borrower chooses to sell the property, 'negative equity insurance' kicks in that caps the borrower's liability. There are lower mortgage rates on the market place, but this proposition will be attractive to the risk averse.

Nutrasweet communicated their compelling value proposition of ingredient consistency face to face. The company faced the threat that the patent for aspartame (the generic form of Nutrasweet) was expiring. How could the Nutrasweet Company prevent its major customers, like Diet Coke and Diet Pepsi, from specifying lower-priced unbranded aspartames? Rao, Bergen and Davis (2000) give the answer in a *Harvard Business Review* article. In separate meetings with Coca-Cola and Pepsi executives, the company highlighted the negative consequences of such an ingredient switch. To Coca-Cola they explained the consequences of consumers discovering that it had replaced the original Nutrasweet with a cheaper alternative – is it still the real thing? And Nutrasweet committed to informing consumers with media advertising in this situation. Similarly they identified the equivalent threat to the Diet Pepsi brand, if Pepsi downgraded to a generic. It proved a compelling value proposition.

In a retail context, the AA provides breakdown cover. Members whose cars break down on the road can call on the AA patrols to get them on their way again. The AA is the largest operator in the UK market with more patrols and more cars fixed than any other. Inevitably they face lower-priced competition. How do they respond? With an advertisement that states clearly, 'you can buy breakdown cover for less than £39.00 but how much less will you get?' (see Figure 11.1).

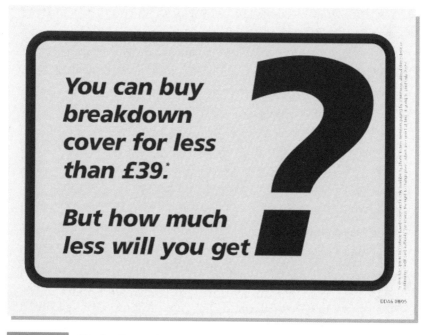

**Figure 11.1** AA advertisement

## Before you buy cheaper cover, check it against the AA.

*Yes, you can get breakdown cover for less than the AA. But before you do, make sure the cover you're buying matches up to the AA.*

**No one has more patrols.**
The AA has more than twice as many patrols on the road as any other breakdown organisation, so there's always one close by. What's more, AA patrols are dedicated professionals – some breakdown organisations rely solely on local garages for roadside repairs.

**No one is better equipped to find you.**
If you break down, the AA has the latest satellite technology to help find the shortest route to get to you.

**Nobody fixes more cars.**
As the UK's largest breakdown organisation, on average we attend a breakdown every 8.7 seconds and repair around 8 out of 10 breakdowns by the roadside.

**No one is better equipped to keep you on the road.**
Only the AA has 'Vixen', a unique on-board computer to help diagnose faults rapidly when you're broken down.

## And will you be getting all this?

**With the AA, you're always covered.**
When you're with the AA, you're covered for breakdowns 24 hours a day, 365 days a year.

**With the AA, you'll know we're on our way.**
Call us from a mobile and we'll text you to keep you updated on how soon a patrol will be with you.

**With the AA, you won't be charged extra for labour.**
You'll never be charged extra for labour carried out at the roadside, no matter how long the repairs take.

**Not sure you'll be getting the same kind of cover? Then give us a call at the AA.**

### AA Breakdown Cover
## 0800 197 4585
### www.theAA.com

Quote ref: 0500

### 3 Show the trade-offs

Customers will also pay more when the trade-offs are explained to them. Buyers tend to underestimate the benefits unless the vendor quantifies them. So the vendor's aim is to raise the knowledge levels of uninformed or unaware buyers so that they are willing to pay more for higher levels of benefit. Nagle and Cressman (2002) give a number of successful examples. A supplier of long-haul trucks quantified the value of features that created driver comfort by demonstrating factually the positive impact on driver retention. A telecom company showed the value of its superior reliability by calculating the revenue loss from service interruptions in their data lines.

Industrial buyers are often more sensitive to quality rather than price because the benefits of regular deliveries and consistent quality help them run their businesses smoothly and profitably. However, they need to be made aware of the trade-offs.

## 4   Show the price step options

Another form of communication is to set out the product range in terms of quality steps, so that the customer can see how they get more when they pay more. The Braun Oral B website explains diagrammatically that its electric toothbrushes come in four levels – entry level, good, better and best (see Table 11.1). The customer can chose to pay more for a higher specification and performance.

**Table 11.1**   Braun Oral B electric toothbrush

| Level | Model | Additional features |
| --- | --- | --- |
| Entry | Battery toothbrush | High speed oscillation<br>Two-minute timer |
| Good | Plaque-control ultra toothbrush | Ultra-speed oscillation plus charging light indicator |
| Better | 3D pulsating toothbrush | Above plus memory, pressure sensor, 3D brushing action |
| Best | 3D Excel pulsating toothbrush | Above plus 3D Excel brushing action, two speeds |

*Source*: www.oralb.com/findit/power.asp.

This approach frequently applies in business-to-business price lists.

## 5   Encourage customer word-of-mouth communications

Positive product and service experience can be a strong reason to pay more. If the vendor is unknown, then it is hard for the buyer to take a sales story on trust. Far greater credibility accrues to another user. Thus many vendors focus on encouraging satisfied customers to pass on their positive views to potential buyers.

The Ritz-Carlton at Battery Park, New York, charges $50 extra for a room with a harbour view. How do they persuade customers to talk about them? Answer: each of these rooms is equipped with a telescope to gaze at the Statue of Liberty. What guest could resist reporting this to his or her friends and colleagues? Industrial equipment manufacturers provide demonstrations at reference sites of satisfied customers. The potential buyer can see the machinery operating and talk to management and operatives about the experience in practice. Other techniques include setting up user groups to share experiences and good practice. Giving advance information of innovations to vocal clients can achieve very effective dissemination – they find it irresistible to show off their knowledge by passing on the information within the industry. Word-of-mouth communication from one customer to a potential customer is a powerful communication device.

## 6  Communication context

The context of communication can enhance the emotional value of a brand. Premium brands may chose to present their messages in colour advertising, rather than black and white. They will select high-quality journals with good production standards. ABB selling power and automation technology conveys its status through poster advertising at international airports. The media context has certain connotations. In the USA, the international brewer, InBev, positions its lead brand, Stella Artois, as a premium product with the slogan 'Perfection has its price'. They use print and posters. According to *Brandweek*, wholesalers urged InBev not to ruin the brand with TV commercials. In the UK, Stella Artois has associated itself with top-level tennis by sponsoring a tournament at Queen's since 1979 – John McEnroe was its first singles winner.

Ford take pains to place newly launched upmarket and sporty models with celebrity early-adopters to influence subsequent uptake.

## 7  Colour cues

Colour can imply certain attributes. Strident colours demand
attention. Calm colours suggest quiet confidence. Table 11.2 shows
how discount airlines, like Air Berlin, bmibaby, EasyJet,
Germanwings, Jet2, Air Polonia, Ryanair, Wizz Air and 20 others
across Europe are selling their wares with a market-trader's pricing
mentality, calling for attention in vivid red, bright orange and
glaring green.

**Table 11.2**    Low-price airlines, bright colours

| | |
|---|---|
| EasyJet | Orange script, orange tailplane |
| Ryanair | Bright yellow stripe between blue and white |
| JET2 | 'JET' shown in bright red |
| Air Berlin | Presented in red capital letters |
| Wizz Air | Pink and purple aircraft |
| Air Polonia | Tail and engine pods in orange and blue |
| Bmibaby | 'Baby' written in red |
| Germanwings | Purple |

By contrast, the leading flag carriers in Europe, British Airways and
Lufthansa, both subscribe to clean white plane livery with a
calming dark blue underside. With dignity and in a calming deep
blue, British Airways offer their advantages.

The quiet confidence is further supported in press advertising.
Under a headline 'Nice and nicer', which promoted flights to Nice
in France, British Airways brings out the benefit side of the value
proposition. It states that advertised prices are for return flights –
implicitly discrediting misleading one-way price deals. In addition,
the company points out that all its flights are from centrally
located airports, knowing that for weekend trips a two-hour coach
journey can subtract significant enjoyment from a low price.
Memories of discomfort can remain long after the discount is
forgotten. British Airways goes on to add that flights are frequent
and at civilized times, seats are allocated, and food and drink is
complimentary.

8  **Sound and smell of quality**

Customers are willing to pay more when they draw quality connotations from sensory cues. For example, Volvo cars pay close attention to the operation of switches and controls used by the driver. Firm and convincing 'clicks' leave an impression of durable construction. The scent of leather as a shoebox is opened, the subtle aroma of new-mown grass pumped through a gardening store's air-conditioning can help sell upscale goods.

This technique is not restricted to consumer markets. Industrial detergents include a smell of pine or lemon for a psychological lift in effectiveness. The smooth movement of indicator dials and the quality of paint finish are deployed to present machinery in a favourable light.

9  **Pricing theatre**

Finally, pricing itself can provide entertainment value that gives a brand a premium standing. For example, Yo Sushi restaurants use price to create an element of theatre: five different plate colours indicate price levels, from low-cost blue to expensive purple plated dishes. Digital price boards can vary the prices during the day, and founder Simon Woodroffe is talking of allowing customers in the financial district to buy Sushi 'futures'!

Wisdom Health Lab, a health food shop in Airlie Beach, Queensland, Australia, offers a breakfast menu with a fixed charge. The cost is A$7.75 if you arrive for breakfast at 7.45a.m. and the price rises by 25 cents every 15 minutes. The time you order is the price you pay – a fun way of encouraging people to get up earlier in the morning! What time will you be up?

# Iffy invoicing – throwing advantages away

Having persuaded your customer to pay more, there is a danger zone of doubt. It comes with the arrival of the invoice. The invoice itself is a piece of communication. As such it should reinforce the impression of good value that has been painstakingly built up. Often it does not. Poor practice affects consumer markets and industrial transactions. For many subscribers to telecommunications services, the monthly bill is the only regular contact. It can easily be the largest source of complaints. Geoff Nairn (2004), writing in the *Financial Times* quotes Verizon, the US local carrier who recently designed its phone bills to make them easier to read for its 30 million US customers. Verizon admitted that its old bill had become complicated and hard to follow. Early customers of 3, the wireless operator in the UK, complained that they could not understand their bills – the company soon moved to a simpler tariff.

Worse than obfuscation is inaccuracy. AT&T admits that a few years ago its billing systems had errors of 15 percent. New practices have improved matters considerably. Executional shortfalls in invoicing can delay payment and jeopardize the brand reputation that earns a premium price. The billing system must be accurate and the invoice must appear straightforward and simple for customers to understand.

**Action:** Sample check a range of invoices for accuracy, clarity and ease of comprehension. Ask yourself if your invoices reflect and support your brand values?

# Take a bravery pill – announce a price increase

Companies are reluctant to announce price increases for three reasons. Customers may protest or even reduce purchases, staff may be apprehensive in communicating and negotiating and the news is likely to receive unfavourable media coverage. Yet successful price increases can contribute more effectively to the bottom line than any other factor. So what are the golden rules for success? What is best practice?

1 **Understand your customers.** How has their ability to pay changed over recent times? What factors will influence their willingness to pay? Buoyant demand and positive success in their market place will make negotiations easier. Helping customers to succeed with their own customers, supports pushing through a price increase. Be associated with their success.

2 **Custom and practice.** If the price leader operates a fixed date increase, then follow the pattern. Companies with a convention of an annual price increase expected by customers and notified

substantially ahead of time have an advantage over companies in markets where increases are more random and individually negotiated. As inflation has reduced over the early years of the twenty-first century, it has become more difficult to maintain regular price increases. Yet if a company is able to maintain the pattern, increases will be easier to achieve.

**3 Pick the best time.** Look at your customers' calendars – price increases near the end of their financial year are likely to be resisted more strongly if it may inhibit expected year-end profits. When is the peak selling season? Price increases are easier to achieve as market demand is rising.

**4 Testing the market.** In industrial markets it can be hard to determine the true scope for a price increase. Perhaps vocal salespeople will caution against a rise for fear of reducing their bonuses. Customers may make empty threats. Who knows what is best. Customer research can give the answer. Not by asking customers' opinions – you know the answer they'd give! Rather by selecting six to ten customers who typify the bulk of the market, big enough to be representative, not so big as to threaten the company success if business is lost. Research means preparing and actually negotiating the desired rate of price increase with these customers. The outcome of the negotiations determines the price increase strategy for the rest of the customers.

**5 Be scientific and specific.** Where value is being delivered to customers with a strong customer surplus, increase prices boldly. Where the surplus is smaller, increase at a lower rate. Where customer resistance is well-founded hold prices. Where value to customers has diminished, consider price reductions. Review segmentation for opportunities to increase margins through higher prices to less price-sensitive groups, and increase volumes from price-sensitive segments by lowering prices, without encouraging sales leakage between the segments. An across the board increase may be the wrong approach. Smart pricing is about capturing value.

6 **Take costs out of the system before seeking an increase.** John Zeally, managing partner of Accenture's European consumer goods practice, is quoted by Claire Murphy in *Marketing Magazine* (2005), 'Manufacturers that have been able to demonstrate to retailers that they have worked hard to cut costs out of their system will be reaping the rewards as retailers will be more open to considering price increases.'

7 **Show benefits linked to an increase.** Present an increase at the same time as a new benefit or make a commitment to invest in an aspect that will improve the experience or service for the customer. It sounds better than presenting a price increase as the same as yesterday only more expensive.

8 **Dangers of linking price increases to raw material price increases.** In 2005, steel, titanium and other commodity prices rose as a result of demand expansion in China. It was tempting to present the cost increases to customers and simply add an index for raw materials. Tempting, but wrong. What goes up, must come down. Any increase today will be met with a future demand for a reduction. Pricing is best seen as a reflection of value in the market place, rather than a summation of all the costs of production. Pricing should be market driven, not cost plus.

Negate a competitor's advantage. If there are underlying cost increases affecting competitors as well then it may be worth highlighting that rivals will either have to pass on the increase or damage the integrity of their supply.

9 **Go beyond the buyer.** Where the buyer is adamant that no increase is possible, go further. Philips successfully presented industrial lighting to human resource managers with details of the motivational impact of natural daylight bulbs. These had been rejected previously by facilities managers, intent on holding down costs irrespective of benefits.

In the case of dairy farmers in the UK, intransigent buyers from supermarkets rejected price increases for milk. The farmers took the issue over the head of the young buyers from Tesco. They took it to the Chief Executive and the shareholders. On Friday 13 June 2003, they protested outside the Royal Lancaster Hotel where the Annual General Meeting was taking place. Placards read: 'Tesco profits, farmers squeezed', 'Who's creaming it?' 'Farmers paid 9p per pint. Shopper pays . . .', 'Cheap food, 11 farmers go bust every day, 1 commits suicide every week.' They highjacked the Tesco slogan 'Every little helps' and using the same font paraded the slogan, 'Tesco – Every little hurts'. This and other protests gained public attention over time. Maggie Urry (2005), writing in the *Financial Times*, quoted Billy Keane, Finance Director of Robert Wiseman Dairies, saying that when the group went to supermarket customers asking for a price increase, it found it was 'pushing against an open door'. Retailers were mindful of the negative publicity they had suffered and they realized putting a tight squeeze on suppliers could prove counter-productive.

10 **Be confident.** Many companies try to minimize communication about price increases and hope that quietly slipping in an increase with an anonymous press release will minimize resistance. An alternative view is that clear communication fronted by a senior person can achieve positive results. There is a benefit from confidently asserting that prices must rise, giving ample notice and a valid rationale. Transparent behaviour can also encourage competitors to respect the upward price movement and respond with their own increases.

Marn, Roegner and Zawada (2004) recommend reinforcing price-increase messages consistently with a deliberate and structured communications plan. This might begin with internal briefings. Meetings with customers face to face would follow to make them aware of the state of the industry. An article could be placed in the industry journal on trends and patterns. Next the website would carry a notification of overall price trend information. The increase date would be announced in a formal letter explaining the rationale. Analysts would be briefed so reports of the increase could circulate through financial contacts. Finally, the detailed price increase would be communicated and a new price list would appear on the website.

If customers are always looking for deals and holding back on buying until they get them, it may not be the price that is too high. Another explanation is that suppliers have taught them that this behaviour is always rewarded with better terms. If this is the case, the urgent need is to recover price integrity. Some deals will have to be lost in order to demonstrate that the price is real and will be upheld. Walking away may be a costly action in the short term but a lucrative long-term strategy.

Finally, where there are long-term contracts in place, there is still a role for price communications. Announcing that you are *not* increasing prices can convey good value and draw positive attention to the agreed price. Scottish Power wrote to customers on capped price contracts when a rival announced a price increase. Their aim was to remind customers that they were in the right place. Part of price communication is reassurance to support long-term loyalty.

## How to increase prices paid, without imposing a price increase

In some industries with price-aggressive competitors and markets with powerful customers, it can be extremely difficult to command price increases. It is worth challenging these pessimistic assumptions initially. If the conditions are validated, then other tactics come into play. The UK wine retailing business is ultra-competitive with price pressures from off-licences and supermarkets. Majestic Wine Warehouse increased its profits year on year, not by increasing list prices, but by persuading its customers to trade up to higher-quality wines. In 2005 their average bottle price was up from £5.40 to £5.51. Smart pricing means increasing prices paid, without putting through a formal price increase.

How can you do this? There are a number of techniques:

1 Revise discount structure.

2 Amend the discount scale, adding interim steps – why must steps move in multiples of 5 percent?

3 Reduce promotional allowances.

4 Raise minimum order levels.

**5** Add a delivery charge.

**6** Identify repairs carried out during regular servicing and charge for the repair.

**7** Make an installation charge.

**8** Charge for inspection and safety certification.

**9** Standard charges apply to standard delivery only – make extra charges for rush orders.

**10** Introduce charges for customers using help-lines by using premium rate phone lines.

**11** Trade customers up to higher specification versions.

**12** Produce less low-margin items so there is better availability on high-margin lines and any stock-outs occur with low-margin products. This may even encourage some trading up.

**13** Negotiate penalty clauses for late delivery and agree a bonus for early completion at the same time. Then deliver early.

**14** Link contracts to activity levels in the industry, so that higher activity drives prices upwards.

**15** Study buying processes in detail to discover the level at which buyers compare prices with your competitors. Create price structures and discount scales that favour you. For example include early payment allowance within the normal discount scale (where the comparison needs to favour you) and then add a late payment penalty (where no comparison is made).

## Price-cut perils

It is always assumed that price increases are bad news and everyone loves a price cut. Not so, as pub chain J. D. Wetherspoons found out. Facing price cuts from supermarkets on beers, J. D. Wetherspoons dropped its bar prices. Where the supermarkets had been praised for offering better value for money, the pub chain was lambasted for encouraging binge drinking! With price changes, the critical aspect is managing the communications in your favour.

# Chapter takeaways

- Nine answers to the question, 'Why pay more?'
  - genuinely better product, clearly communicated
  - highlight the risks, provide reassurance
  - show the trade-offs customers are making with lower prices
  - give customers price steps for better specifications and let them choose
  - encourage customers word-of-mouth recommendation – they can sell premium prices better than you
  - create the appropriate quality context for communications
  - use colour association to convey quality
  - use sensory cues like touch, sound and smell to shape perceptions
  - seek opportunities for pricing theatre and entertainment.
- You need accurate billing systems and invoices that customers can understand.
- How to announce price increases – ten best practices.
- How to increase prices without a price increase – 14 ways to obtain a better margin.

# Management questions for your business

- How could we combine tangible factors and emotional cues to boost willingness to pay?
- The danger zone of doubt – are we proud of our invoicing? Are invoices accurate, simple and understandable?
- There are best practices for price increase announcements – how many do we use?
- Where can we grow our customer margins without a formal price increase?

# Going further – references and additional reading

Beirne, M. and Hein, K. (2004) 'InBev chases US market with huge war chest', *Brandweek*, 6 December.

Blythman, J. (2005) *Shopped: the Shocking Power of British Supermarkets*, Harper Perennial, London.

Braun: www.oralb.com/findit/power.asp – steps of quality in Braun tooth-brushes.

Budden, R. (2005) 'Now even mortgage lenders have an answer for everything', *Financial Times*, 18 June.

Cohen, A. (2005) 'Real ale and rooftop pools can make your trip worthwhile – extras to look for in an hotel', *The Times*, 27 June.

*The Economist* (2005) 'Monkey business sense – monkeys show the same irrational aversion to risks as humans', 25 June.

Howze, J. 'Tried and tested: Heinz souped up new soups', i.village.co.uk/food

Lawrence, F. (2004) 'Heinz gives soup a healthier recipe', *Guardian*, 26 August.

Marketing Society Awards for Excellence 2005, *Marketing Magazine*, June.

Marn, M. V., Roegner, E. V. and Zawada, C. C. (2004) *The Price Advantage*, Wiley, Hoboken, NJ.

Murphy, C. (2005) 'Rising costs? Please pass it on', *Marketing Magazine,* March.

Nagle, T. T. and Cressman, G. E. (2002) 'Don't just set prices, manage them', *Marketing Management,* November/December.

Nairn, G. (2004) 'Nimble billing for launch of services', *Financial Times*, 14 April.

Rao, A. R., Bergen, N. E., and Davis, S. (2000) 'How to fight a price war', *Harvard Business Review*, March.

Urry, M. (2005) 'Rise in milk prices eases pressure on farmers', *Financial Times*, 18 April.

Winkler, J. (1983) *Pricing for Results*, Heinemann, London.

Young, R. (2004) 'Heinz cans its fat soup for a healthy variety', *The Times*, 26 August.

part

# Pricing success and executive summary

# 12

## Pricing success – keeping discipline, measuring results

### Higher prices (but higher discounts)

Smarter pricing needs every player in the pricing decision to share a common strategy. All too often, different players have divergent aims and aspirations. Top management such as managing directors and finance directors may not see pricing opportunities in the same light as trade negotiators or brand managers.

Top management, for example, reflects revenue and profit aspirations in its targeted prices. It considers the level of market inflation with data and forecasts from company economists and will be aware of indices of raw materials and labour costs. With an eye to shareholders' expectations, it is eager to grow margins. Often it will place more reliance on hard facts – such as raw material costs or current competitor prices – than softer assumptions about customers' willingness or reluctance to pay more. For this reason they may be bullish about pricing targets.

By contrast, the sales force is often focused on short-term targets of sales volume or share of major customer purchases. Its view of pricing reflects the need to win the business. Trade promotions flex pricing strategies in order to achieve short-term volume targets. Its daily contact is with customers. Procurement teams deprecate quality arguments, challenge price increases, demand discounts and threaten to buy elsewhere. For this reason salespeople may be pessimistic about pricing targets.

Marketing managers and brand managers will consider the strategies of brand competitors and opportunities of consumer insights in order to position brands appropriately. Their recommendations, based on soft factors, may seem inconsequential compared with the hard facts of material cost increases and tough negotiating buyers. It appears that marketers are having less influence in pricing decisions than in the 1990s. The real action occurs in Finance and Sales.

So what happens when management's desire for margin increases conflicts with the sales team's aim to win the deal? 'We want higher prices' versus 'we cannot put our prices up'. Robert J. Dolan and Hermann Simon (1996) offer a plausible view that list prices rise . . . but so do discounts! They describe a chemical company whose list prices rose by 22 percent over four years. At the same time, the sales force increased the level of existing discounts and even created new discounts. The net result was that actual prices paid only increased by 3.5 percent. The bulk of the list price increases had been discounted away.

Three conclusions can be drawn:

1  Pricing decisions and execution must be co-ordinated across functions.

2  Price discipline is vital to achieve results in practice.

3  Price measurement should be based on prices actually paid rather than notional list prices.

We will look first at price co-ordination and second at discount management and finally at measurement for success.

## Co-ordinating pricing decisions – how does it happen?

Top management and three functions – finance, sales and marketing – all have a part to play in pricing decisions. The extent of that involvement could range from the ability to express a view all the way to decision-making authority. The role will vary between companies and according to circumstances. In orderly and slow-changing environments, time is available for a consultative approach. In the urgent midst of a price war, single-minded decisiveness is likely to prevail.

Dolan and Simon (1996) offer three scenarios used in practice to achieve functional co-ordination.

- Internal negotiation. Finance and sales determine their own views for price movements and then representatives meet to share opinions with the task of reaching a consensus that will be recommended to general management. The analysis and the subsequent debate should bring out all the relevant factors. A consensus should result in agreement of the major players to make the agreed strategy succeed. However, this approach is also subject to political power plays.

- Multi-functional teams. A cross-functional team is established to assess pricing requirements and develop a single proposal. This focus on a unified approach should mean less conflict. It may, however, lack the detailed pricing depth of departmental submissions. It can be a time-consuming process.

- Pricing manager or specialist reporting to general management. This approach is appearing in a number of industries. However, the success depends on the knowledge and credibility of the individual. This may come under challenge from the sales and finance executives.

In industrial markets, pricing committees of up to ten members facilitate price planning. Research by Richard Lancioni (2005) indicates that 68 percent of industrial companies use this approach. He found that the functions of the committees varied from company to company, but generally they include responsibility for developing pricing strategies (58 percent), administering those strategies (88 percent) and addressing and analyzing competitive threats in markets (87 percent). A minority decide new product pricing (27 percent) and sales incentive programmes (12 percent).

A strong recommendation of Marn, Roegner and Zawada (2004) is that pricing is owned by an executive champion within each business unit. This champion would lead a specialized pricing group. In their view, the role of the group is to make actual pricing performance visible and continuously look for untapped opportunities to do even better.

**Action:** Strong co-ordination is necessary to achieve a unified approach.

# Sales force giving it away?

In industrial markets, buyers may not accept the set list prices and expect to negotiate. Specifications may vary according to buyers' needs. The logic follows that the salespeople should carry out the negotiations. They are most familiar with the relevant benefits provided to the buyer and the value to their business. This knowledge should achieve maximum value capture. In addition, allowing the salesperson to negotiate discounts enables the deal to be closed on the spot and permits rapid responses to changing market conditions. It sounds positive.

There are positive aspects: sales negotiations are time efficient, preferred by customers who feel they are obtaining an individual deal and the authority can be motivational to salespeople. However, there are four dangers:

1    The salesperson's success in selling depends on the agreement on terms and hence the temptation may be to secure the deal with a lower price. In an example quoted by Sodhi and Sodhi (2005) in *Harvard Business Review*, sales representatives at a manufacturer of industrial equipment with authority to invoice at $81,000 gave further unauthorized discounts taking the price down to $75,000.

2    Salespeople frequently over-estimate the price-sensitivity of their customers. Firms segmenting their customers into price-buyers, convenience-buyers and quality-buyers find that salespeople place many more customers in the price-sensitive segment than actually belong there.

3    Different salespeople may negotiate different prices for similar specifications. The increasing transparency of prices across buying groups, or as a result of buyers changing firms, means that inconsistencies come to light and the levelling that results is almost

invariably downward. Take-overs are a particular threat. If one customer takes over another smaller customer and discovers that the smaller company had secured better terms, they may demand retrospective rebates from the supplier.

4 Sales people may not always be aware of the internal cost implications of the terms they agree. These costs can have a detrimental impact on margins.

Rarely do sales people have total autonomy over price and most will have authority within guidelines. The right extent of authority depends on the industry complexity and the variation between customers and the skill and knowledge level of salespeople. If there is discretion over terms it is vital that a regular review of negotiated discounts takes place. This would normally map sales value or volume against prices. You would expect larger customers to receive better terms. Exceptions need questioning.

In Figure 12.1, the customers above the dotted line are receiving better terms than their volume appears to justify. A review would investigate the history and reasoning behind these discounts. Is this a distinct

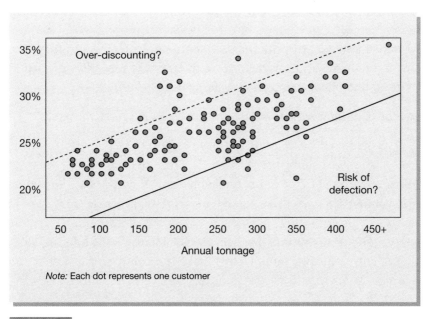

**Figure 12.1** Discount review: terms by volume

segment? How likely are these terms to come to the notice of larger customers? How could they be justified to other customers? How might the terms be brought in line?

The customers below the solid line are receiving worse terms than their volume suggests. Are these customers at risk of defection if the disparity comes to their attention?

**Action:** Map actual discounts against volume sales and review all customers outside the expected band.

In practice, reviews of actual discounts will normally result in tightening authority levels. Less delegation of authority tends to result in greater profitability. Sodhi and Sodhi (2005) describe the results of the review that took place at a global manufacturer of industrial equipment in their article 'Six sigma pricing'. For transactions between $100,000 and $150,000 in a particular market, sales representatives could offer any discount up to 30 percent on their own authority. To offer a lower price they would need to gain the approval of a price analyst who would check guideline prices by product, region and transaction size and could authorize up to 35 percent discount. To go to 40 percent would need the pricing manager's sign off. Higher still needed top management agreement. The guidelines and the escalation process were clear and operated rapidly. List price increases were implemented and thanks to the tighter controls from the review, the increase was fully reflected in bottom-line prices – annual revenues grew by $5.8 million.

**Action:** Consider reduction of authority levels for greater profit.

Salespeople paid on commission have an incentive to perform. If the commission is volume-based, then the incentive encourages them to discount in order to maximize total volumes. Most firms base incentives on volume because these figures are readily available and easy to measure. Incentivizing salespeople by profit contribution is more relevant. Putting this into practice poses challenges – the information is less readily available, more factors make it a complex calculation and margin confidentiality is compromised.

Nagle and Holden (2002) propose that salespeople are given sales goals where these goals are set at 'target prices'. If they sell at prices above the target, then their sales credit is adjusted by the improvement in profit and, conversely if they achieve prices below the target level their sales credit is reduced proportionately.

**Action:** Review sales incentives and focus rewards on profitable behaviour.

The three best practices for achieving profitable results from sales forces with discount negotiating authority are accurate knowledge of actual discounts, controlled authority levels and incentives based on contribution.

## Managing pricing discipline

In consumer markets, there are pressures to discount or 'promote' products. Consumers respond to promotions. Retail channels encourage promotions and discounts to enhance store interest. Branded goods manufacturers are under great pressure to promote. Yet before promotions are created, manufacturers need to take account of two factors: the price elasticity or expandability of their category (will people buy more if the price goes down?) and the brand equity or reputation. Considering these factors could reduce the promotional discounts where value is given away unnecessarily.

McKinsey consultants, Davey, Childs and Carlotti (1998) state that a brand with a high reputation in an expandable category, for example a brand-leading snack product, should have a wide price band. The wide band extends from the normal high price reflecting equity to an occasional deep discount, targeted at bring in new users. A measure of high brand equity is that buyers of B-brands will trade up when the A-brand is promoted, but buyers of the A-brand do not trade down when the B-brand rival is on promotion.

Alternatively, a product in expandable category with less equity, say the B-brand in the market, should use moderate pricing and promotions, and operate in a narrower price band.

Products in a low expandable area with high equity, such as a brand-leading toilet paper or detergent, need a very narrow price band. These brands should use promotions sparingly because these will not bring in any new business, simply time-shift existing purchases.

**Action:** Determine the expandability of sales in your category and the relative brand reputation to determine the ideal width of the price band.

# Prevent profit leakage

Uncontrolled or unnecessary discounts are only one form of profit leakage. Allowances also transfer value from supplier to customer. Consider the increasing power of European supermarkets, whose demands for supplier allowances is mushrooming. Investigative food journalist Joanna Blythman (2005) gives many instances of required or requested payments in her book, *Shopped: the Shocking Power of British Supermarkets*:

- pre-condition for being listed
- for better display positions
- for increasing range or depth of distribution
- for promotions
- retrospective discounts if sales fail to reach projected volumes
- payments to cover product wastage
- requested buybacks of unsold products
- contribution to costs of store refurbishment.

Looking only at average discounts and invoiced terms understates the full extent of all allowances. McKinsey consultants Michael Marn and Robert Rosiello (1992) have called this effect the 'Pocket price waterfall'.

From the dollar list price, order size discounts and competitive discounts are typically applied to produce the invoiced price. It is at this price that organizations normally measure price performance. As we have seen, further allowances are deducted: payment terms allowance, annual volume bonus, off-invoice promotions, co-operative advertising allowances and so on. The final net price is the 'pocket price'.

Examples from Marn and Rosiello (1992) include a pocket price 16.7 percent below invoiced price for a consumer packaged goods company, 17.7 percent below for a commodity chemical company and 28.9 percent below for a lighting products supplier. It is at the pocket price that valid pricing measurement should be carried out. Yet accounting systems hide the customer specific figures in general budgets – co-operative advertising funds are often incorporated in overall advertising budgets, emergency freight costs for one customer will be lost among other business transportation expenses. These hidden costs must be pulled out so that true margins are explicit.

**Action:** Understand the precise 'pocket price' by identifying all customer specific costs and allocating them so that individual customer profitability can be clearly seen. This may result in decisions to expand business with higher margin segments and renegotiate or walk away from low-margin customers.

## When 'strategic' really means loss-making

Understanding customer profitability at 'pocket price' level will identify some accounts that cost more to serve than the contribution they provide. Typically they are large accounts that have forcefully negotiated low prices and high allowances. They demand extra support, require immediate delivery and tailored product variations. Payment terms are stretched to their benefit. We label these accounts 'strategic customers'. We claim that they bring status to us, that they give value as reference accounts, that they influence other buyers. Professor Robert J. Dolan (1995) calls them 'the dangerous strategic accounts' in his *Harvard Business Review* article. In fact, 'strategic' is a euphemism for loss-making. Is it smart to subsidize big players by charging more to small customers? Maybe the answer is yes, maybe it is no, but the question should be asked.

**Action:** Challenge the assumption that you *must* sell to 'strategic customers'.

# How do you measure success?

Measuring pricing success is challenging. Using measures like volume sales growth and market share gains may demonstrate that prices are right ... or that they are too low, leaving money on the table. Measuring improvement in margin or contribution could mean that prices are right ... or that they are too high, failing to make profitable sales available in the market. So what is the correct measure?

In theory, the true determinant of pricing success is the small size of the sum of money left on the table. The perfect price captures just less than the full value provided to the customer, leaving a small bonus or 'customer surplus' such that they feel they have made a beneficial transaction. It is part economics, part psychology. And both customer economics and psychological perceptions will move as market dynamics change, as new products appear and as competitors increase or reduce prices. What is the practical answer?

The answer is to measure the customers' behaviours that illustrate their estimation of value.

A colleague reminisced about his experience of providing funding for infrastructure developments to governments in developing Asian countries. 'Only twice in my career were deals accepted at the first meeting', he said, 'and at that moment I knew that I had seriously under-priced them!'

## 1. The 'look to book' ratio

The first key indicator is the 'Look to Book' ratio. What proportion of potential customers, who ask for a quotation, go on to place the order? How many enquirers follow on to make the purchase? If the strike rate is rising, the price may be too low. If the strike rate is falling, the price may be too high.

## 2. The sound of silence

Customers will complain vociferously if prices are too high. Listen for the sound of silence. Few grumbles about price may suggest that prices are too low.

## 3. The switching rate

The third key indicator is the switching rate. What percentage of last year's customers are not buying this year? How many existing customers have switched to other suppliers? If the churn rate of customers is declining, the price may be too low. If the churn rate is rising, then the price may be too high. If sales information by customer is not available, for example at a retailer, it can be possible to research sample groups of customers to establish this information at a macro-level.

## 4. Market share movement

The fourth indicator is holding market share. Sodhi and Sodhi (2005) describe how an industrial equipment manufacturer monitored pricing effectiveness with a monthly review. Vice-presidents of marketing, sales and finance, and their direct reports scrutinized pricing performance by region and transaction size. Specifically they looked for increasing average transaction value (to meet agreed internal objectives), fewer pricing exceptions to the scale of guidelines and finally to a maintenance of market share. If share is being lost to comparable competitors, then prices may be too high. If share is being gained from these competitors, then prices may be too low. An exception is where pricing is being deployed as part of a corporate aim to grow market share. In this instance, the consistency of share growth is the indicator.

## 5. Fixed costs per unit sold

The fifth indicator is an internal ratio looking at fixed costs per unit sold. Eugster, Kakkar and Roegner (2000), writing in the *McKinsey Quarterly*, recommend this as a further way of assessing a market. They suggest that a decreasing fixed cost per unit sold is a sign of prices that are too low. Conversely, an increasing fixed cost per unit sold could warn that prices are too high. In their view lack of quick pricing or volume swings show that prices are at an optimal rate.

# Difficult but important

Smarter pricing is difficult and that is good news. Easy things can be replicated by competitors: addressing difficult things brings you big advantages. People who roll up their sleeves rarely lose their shirts. Success in pricing comes from rolling up your sleeves, considering a wide range of factors, and managing them carefully and consistently. It does not come from getting one big thing right.

Smarter pricing needs time and attention. You must combine customer insight, competitive context, a clear view of strategic aims and a solid knowledge of tools and techniques. You need informed judgement. You need confidence in the product's ability to command a premium price justified by the value it provides to the customer. Most of all, smarter pricing demands a sound understanding of the attitudes and emotions that make a customer willing to pay.

# Chapter takeaways

- Price decisions must be co-ordinated across the functions of a company lest the potential profit from higher list prices is simply passed on in increased discounts.

- In business-to business achieving profitable results from sales forces with discount negotiating authority needs accurate knowledge of actual discounts, controlled authority levels and incentives based on contribution.

- In consumer markets, the width of the price band and the extent of promotional pricing depends on the expandability of the sector and the brand reputation.

- Measure price performance at the 'Pocket price' level, taking into account all discounts, over-riders, rebates and allowances.

- Pricing success is measured not simply by rising sales or rising margins, but through a mix of monitors: potential customer strike rate, existing customer switching rate, maintenance of market share and steady ratio of fixed costs per unit.

# Management questions for your business

- Are finance, sales, marketing and top management all committed to the same view of pricing? What is our co-ordinating mechanism?
- What does our volume discount map show?
- What are our authority levels for sales discount decisions?
- Do sales incentives reinforce profitable decisions?
- How wide are our price bands?
- Do we monitor customer profitability at 'pocket price' level?
- Should we do business with unprofitable 'strategic accounts'?
- How do we measure our pricing effectiveness?

# Going further – references and additional reading

Blythman, J. (2005) *Shopped: the Shocking Power of British Supermarkets*, Harper Perennial, London.

Davey, K. K. S., Childs, A. and Carlotti, S. J. (1998) 'Why your price band is wider than it should be', *McKinsey Quarterly*, 3.

Dolan, R. J. (1995) 'How do you know when the price is right?', *Harvard Business Review*, September.

Dolan, R. and Simon, H. (1996) *Power Pricing*, The Free Press, New York, NY.

Eugster, C. E., Kakkar, J. N. and Roegner, E. V. (2000) 'Bringing discipline to pricing', *McKinsey Quarterly*, 1 – see exhibit 4.

Lancioni, R. A. (2005) 'A strategic approach to industrial product pricing: the pricing plan', *Industrial Marketing Management*, 34.

Marn, M., Roegner, E. V. and Zawada, C. C. (2004) *The Price Advantage*, Wiley, Hoboken, NJ.

Marn, M. V. and Rosiello, R. L. (1992) 'Managing price gaining profit', *Harvard Business Review*, September–October.

Nagle, T. T. and Holden, R, K. (2002) *The Strategy and Tactics of Pricing*, Prentice Hall, Upper Saddle River, NJ – see Chapter 8, 'Value-based sales and negotiation'.

Sodhi, M. S. and Sodhi, N. S. (2005) 'Six sigma pricing', *Harvard Business Review*, May.

# 13

# Smarter pricing – the five-minute version

**Some of your prices are too low.** Some customers would pay more, and at some times and places you could charge more. But none of your customers will tell you this. Though they are all too ready and eager to tell you when your prices are too high. And your competitors will harangue your customers with promises of lower prices, and besiege you with price wars. How can you build profits under these conditions? The answer is smarter pricing.

**Finding the smarter price has greater impact on market success than any other element.** One percent on price has more effect than a one percent cost reduction or a one percent volume increase. Yet experts confirm that pricing is often guesswork – a mixture of voodoo and bingo.

**Smarter pricing begins by understanding that the customer is trading money for a combination of product (or service) performance and an emotional association.** Despite claims that a low price is the most important factor, customers actually seek value. Higher perceived benefits will justify a higher price on a value equivalence line and there are six potential ways to build perceptions of superior value. The value proposition defines the package of benefits and price for a target customer group. Focus on the target group: what do they need? What can they afford? Answering these questions can generate opportunities for value innovation.

**Smarter pricing discovers what the market will bear.** Dumb pricing looks at costs and adds a margin. But costs are an internal matter and cost-based prices are unlikely to capture a fair share of the potential value in the market place. Dumb pricing looks at competitors and imitates them. But reactive pricing commoditizes your offering. It disregards differentiation and the unique value you can create for your buyer.

**Identifying what the market will bear is no easy matter.** When customers hear the question, 'How much would you pay for that?' they shift into bargaining mode and produce opening offers that are well beneath their likely real-world behaviour. Pricing research strives to disguise the obviousness of the question, using techniques like trade-off analysis and discrete choice modelling. Sometimes a better way is live price experiments with real customers, tracking price acceptance and price rejection to determine the optimum level.

**Smarter pricing means finding the optimum combination of price and volume.** To do this you must understand the price sensitivity of customers and focus on all the ways to diminish that sensitivity. Some customers have more sensitivity to price, others less. A single average price will be less than some buyers are willing to pay and you forgo value. An average price will also be above the maximum for others and so potential sales will be lost. The answer is price discrimination where prices differ between customers. Segmenting customers by their price sensitivity creates scope for capturing more of the value.

**Pricing can also shape customers' behaviours for the worse or for the better.** Smarter pricing can stimulate particular responses that achieve profitable behaviours, like discouraging waste and encouraging consumption and repeat purchasing.

**Smarter pricing also positions the brand, showing what it stands for relative to competitors, signalling a point of difference** (like accessibility, easy to do business with, reassuring, exclusive, indulgent). Offering relevant differentiation is critical. Higher prices linked to that differentiation can even increase sales.

**You are under threat from value players who seek to undermine you with low price banners. Smarter pricing says do not cede, nor attack on price.** Better to call on a menu of ten strategies to reinforce core values that defend your position. Some price-sensitive customers may defect. Prices may need to be trimmed to continue to deliver value. And profit will come from the level of premium that these strategies deliver.

**Smarter pricing can survive a price war.** Dramatic price cuts make sense only in rare circumstances where latent demand can be released. In most cases price wars destroy value, companies and careers. They can be avoided or mitigated by careful planning and preparedness. Some can be stopped before they start. Thoughtful responses can reduce their effect – non-price responses and selective price actions for example. Put all the deterrent strategies in place. And hope.

**Setting the smarter price is a three-stage process.** It considers:

- Customer factors such as value received, ability and willingness to pay.
- Competitive factors such as the impact the price will have on rivals and how it may influence their behaviour.
- Company factors such as the actual and desired role in the industry, the target positioning in the market place and the life-cycle strategy (premium, skimming or penetration). Finally, a check to ensure the proposed price provides an adequate financial return.

Quantity discounts, multi-dimensional terms and time-based structures can increase revenues and profits. Smart price structures move customers up price stairways. Bundling can achieve the same.

**Smarter price communication answers the question 'Why pay more?'** It uses all the cues of numbering, signalling, reference pricing and price guarantees. Eight communications strategies convey superior benefits, some on technical merit, others using context and intangible indicators. Smarter pricing avoids the danger zone of doubt brought on by accounting obfuscation. And it confidently finds ways to increase prices.

**Smarter pricing brings success through keeping discipline and measuring results.** It co-ordinates all the functions for a unified approach. Authority levels keep control of discounts, product promotions happen within the narrowest price band, and all allowances and off-invoice extras are included in the 'pocket price'. There are no loss-making 'strategic customers'. Smarter pricing is measured by five tests: look-to-book, the sound of silence, the switching rate, market share movement and fixed costs per unit sold.

**Smarter pricing comes from considering a wide range of factors, and managing them carefully and consistently.** It does not come from getting one big thing right. You need informed judgement and a confidence in the product's ability to command a premium price that is justified by the value it provides to the customer.

# 14

# The last word on price

There is one unusual circumstance where customers voluntarily pay over the odds. Satisfied with service in a restaurant, a diner may willingly leave €100 in payment for a bill for €90.

Dr Michael Lynn (1993) of the Cornell School of Hotel Administration has made a personal study of tipping behaviour in the USA, where restaurant patrons fork out $16 billion per year in gratuities. He has discerned patterns of behaviour that can lead to higher tips. Actions that increase trust come to the fore. A personal introduction improves tips. Kneeling beside the table to meet customer's eye level is another proven technique. Randomly, 207 dining parties at a Mexican restaurant were split between the waiter standing or squatting at their table when introducing himself to his customers. Average tips were $1.22 higher (from 14.9 percent to 17.5 percent of the bill) with the waiter squatting down next to the table.

Quoted in the *Cornell Chronicle*, Michael Lynn said, 'Tipping is an interesting behaviour because tips are voluntary payments given after services have been rendered. Consumers rarely pay more than necessary for goods and services. Tipping represents a multi-billion dollar exception to this general rule.' Meeting customers' tangible needs and also their emotional needs for trust by treating them with consideration can result in customers voluntarily paying more.

Voluntarily paying a premium for your product is the greatest accolade a customer can award you. To earn that compliment you must deliver value.

When you are confident in the value you are providing you can be sure of your prices: good medicine never goes on sale. That's smart.

## Going further – references and additional reading

Crawford, F. (2000) 'Researcher in consumer behaviour looks at attitudes of gratitude that affect gratuities', *Cornell Chonicle*, 17 August.

Lynn, M. and Mynier, K. (1993) 'Effect of server posture on restaurant tipping', *Journal of Applied Social Psychology*, 23.

Marn, M., Roegner, E. V. and Zawada, C. C. (2004) *The Price Advantage*, Wiley, Hoboken, NJ – see Chapter 1.

# Index